IMMIGRATION IN THE 21ST CENTURY:
POLITICAL, SOCIAL AND ECONOMIC ISSUES

REMOVAL AND EXCLUSION OF FOREIGN NATIONALS

ISSUES AND CONSIDERATIONS

IMMIGRATION IN THE 21ST CENTURY: POLITICAL, SOCIAL AND ECONOMIC ISSUES

Additional books in this series can be found on Nova's website under the Series tab.

Additional e-books in this series can be found on Nova's website under the e-book tab.

IMMIGRATION IN THE 21ST CENTURY:
POLITICAL, SOCIAL AND ECONOMIC ISSUES

REMOVAL AND EXCLUSION OF FOREIGN NATIONALS

ISSUES AND CONSIDERATIONS

DELIA GIBSON
EDITOR

nova publishers
New York

Library of Congress Cataloging-in-Publication Data

ISBN: 978-1-63482-610-5

Published by Nova Science Publishers, Inc. † New York

Contents

PREFACE

This book provides an overview of removing foreign nationals from the United States. It discusses immigration policies and issues on health-related grounds for exclusion; terrorist grounds for exclusion and removal of aliens; and the consequences of criminal activity for immigrants.

Chapter 1 – The ability to remove foreign nationals (aliens) who violate U.S. immigration law is central to the immigration enforcement system. Some lawful migrants violate the terms of their admittance, and some aliens enter the United States illegally, despite U.S. immigration laws and enforcement. In 2012, there were an estimated 11.4 million resident unauthorized aliens; estimates of other removable aliens, such as lawful permanent residents who commit crimes, are elusive. With total repatriations of over 600,000 people in FY2013—including about 440,000 formal removals—the removal and return of such aliens have become important policy issues for Congress, and key issues in recent debates about immigration reform.

The Immigration and Nationality Act (INA) provides broad authority to the Department of Homeland Security (DHS) and the Department of Justice (DOJ) to remove certain foreign nationals from the United States, including unauthorized aliens (i.e., foreign nationals who enter without inspection, aliens who enter with fraudulent documents, and aliens who enter legally but overstay the terms of their temporary visas) and lawfully present foreign nationals who commit certain acts that make them removable. Any foreign national found to be inadmissible or deportable under the grounds specified in the INA may be ordered removed. The INA describes procedures for making and reviewing such a determination, and specifies conditions under which certain grounds of removal may be waived. DHS officials may exercise certain forms of discretion in pursuing removal orders, and certain removable aliens may be eligible for permanent or temporary relief from removal. Certain grounds for removal (e.g., criminal grounds, terrorist grounds) render foreign nationals ineligible for most forms of relief and may make them eligible for more streamlined (expedited) removal processes.

The "standard" removal process is a civil judicial proceeding in which an immigration judge from DOJ's Executive Office for Immigration Review (EOIR) determines whether an alien is removable. Immigration judges may grant certain forms of relief during the removal process (e.g., asylum, cancellation of removal), and the judge's removal decisions are subject to administrative and judicial review. The INA also describes different types of streamlined removal procedures, which generally include more-limited opportunities for relief and grounds for review. In addition, two alternative forms of removal exempt aliens from certain penalties associated with formal removal: voluntary departure (return) and withdrawal of petition for admission. These are often called "returns."

Following an order of removal, an alien is inadmissible for a minimum of five years after the date of the removal, and therefore is generally ineligible to return to the United States during this time period. The period of inadmissibility is determined by the reason for and type of removal. For example, a foreign national ordered removed based on removal proceedings initiated upon the foreign national's arrival is inadmissible for five years, while a foreign national ordered removed after being apprehended within the United States is inadmissible for 10 years. The length of inadmissibility increases to 20 years for an alien's second or subsequent removal order, and is indefinite for a foreign national convicted of an aggravated felony.

Absent additional factors, unlawful presence in the United States is a civil violation, not a criminal offense, and removal and its associated administrative processes are civil proceedings. As such, aliens in removal proceedings generally have no right to counsel (though they may be represented by counsel at their own expense). In addition, because removal is not considered punishment by the courts, Congress may impose immigration consequences retroactively.

There were a record number of removals between FY2009 and FY2013, including 438,421 removals in FY2013. Approximately 71% of the foreign nationals removed were from Mexico. However, during the same time period the number of returns (most of which occur at the Southwest border) decreased to a low of 178,371 in FY2013—the fewest returns since 1968.

Chapter 2 – News of humans infected with Ebola in West Africa, avian influenza in China, polio in the Middle East, and dengue fever in the

Caribbean are examples of reports that heighten concerns about the health screenings of people arriving in the United States. Under current law, foreign nationals who wish to come to the United States generally must obtain a visa and submit to an inspection to be admitted. One of the reasons why a foreign national might be deemed inadmissible is on health-related grounds. The diseases that trigger inadmissibility in the Immigration and Nationality Act (INA) are those communicable diseases of public health significance as determined by the Secretary of Health and Human Services (HHS).

Currently there are seven diseases deemed a communicable disease of public health significance: chancroid, gonorrhea, granuloma inguinale, infectious leprosy, lymphogranuloma venereum, active tuberculosis, and infectious syphilis. Other diseases incorporated by reference are cholera; diphtheria; infectious tuberculosis; plague; smallpox; yellow fever; viral hemorrhagic fevers (Lassa, Marburg, Ebola, Crimean-Congo, South American, and others not yet isolated or named); severe acute respiratory syndrome (SARS); and "[i]nfluenza caused by novel or reemergent influenza viruses that are causing, or have the potential to cause, a pandemic." The INA also renders inadmissible foreign nationals who are not vaccinated against vaccine-preventable diseases. Vaccinations are statutorily required for mumps, measles, rubella, polio, tetanus, diphtheria, pertussis, influenza type B and hepatitis B. Vaccinations against other diseases may also be required if recommended by the Advisory Committee for Immunization Practices (ACIP).

The Centers for Disease Control and Prevention (CDC) in HHS take the lead in protection against communicable diseases among foreign nationals who come to the United States. The CDC are responsible for providing the technical instructions to civil surgeons and panel physicians who conduct medical examinations for immigration purposes. Foreign nationals who are applying for visas at U.S. consulates are tested by in-country physicians who have been designated by the State Department. The physicians enter into written agreements with the consular posts to perform the examinations according to HHS regulations and guidance. Foreign nationals in the United States who are adjusting to legal permanent resident status are tested by civil surgeons designated by U.S. Citizenship and Immigration Services, an agency within the Department of Homeland Security (DHS). CDC, in conjunction with Customs and Border Protection (CBP) in DHS, operates 20 quarantine stations and has health officials on call for all ports of entry.

From an immigration standpoint, an outbreak of an infectious disease places substantial procedural and resource pressures on CBP, which is charged with screening admissions of all travelers at land, sea, and air ports of entry

(POE). CBP officers screened approximately 362 million individuals in FY2013 for admissions into the United States. CBP works in conjunction with the CDC to monitor travelers and attempt to contain any diseases that may be spread by travelers coming from abroad. In the current context of the Ebola outbreak in West Africa, CDC has emphasized exit-based airport screening from areas with Ebola, and not screening at POEs in the United States. At this point, CDC assures that Ebola poses little risk to the U.S. general population.

Congress has acted legislatively on the health-related grounds for exclusion several times in the recent past. Congress also plays an important oversight role, particularly when concerns arise regarding contagious diseases or potential pandemics.

Chapter 3 – The Immigration and Nationality Act (INA) spells out a strict set of admissions criteria and exclusion rules for all foreign nationals who come permanently to the United States as immigrants (i.e., legal permanent residents) or temporarily as nonimmigrants. Notably, any alien who engages in terrorist activity, or is a representative or member of a designated foreign terrorist organization, is generally inadmissible. After the September 11, 2001, terrorist attacks, the INA was broadened to deny entry to representatives of groups that endorse terrorism, prominent individuals who endorse terrorism, and (in certain circumstances) the spouses and children of aliens who are removable on terrorism grounds. The INA also contains grounds for inadmissibility based on foreign policy concerns.

The report of the National Commission on Terrorist Attacks Upon the United States (also known as the 9/11 Commission) concluded that the key officials responsible for determining alien admissions (consular officers abroad and immigration inspectors in the United States) were not considered full partners in counterterrorism efforts prior to September 11, 2001, and as a result, opportunities to intercept the September 11 terrorists were missed. The 9/11 Commission's monograph, *9/11 and Terrorist Travel*, underscored the importance of the border security functions of immigration law and policy.

In the 110th Congress, legislation was enacted to modify the terrorism-related grounds for inadmissibility and removal, as well as the impact that these grounds have upon alien eligibility for relief from removal. The Consolidated Appropriations Act, 2008 (P.L. 110-161) modified certain terrorism-related provisions of the INA, including exempting specified groups from the INA's definition of "terrorist organization" and expanding immigration authorities' waiver authority over the terrorism-related grounds for exclusion. P.L. 110-257 expressly excludes the African National Congress (ANC) from being considered a terrorist organization, and provides immigration authorities the ability to exempt most terrorism-related and criminal grounds for inadmissibility from applying to aliens with respect to activities undertaken in opposition to apartheid rule in South Africa. Immigration reform is an issue in the 111th Congress, and legislative proposals may contain provisions modifying the immigration consequences of terrorism-related activity.

The case of Umar Farouk Abdulmutallab, who allegedly attempted to ignite an explosive device on Northwest Airlines Flight 253 on December 25, 2009, has refocused attention on terrorist screening during the visa process. He was traveling on a multi-year, multiple-entry tourist visa issued to him in June 2008. State Department officials have acknowledged that Abdulmutallab's father came into the Embassy in Abuja, Nigeria, on November 19, 2009, to express his concerns about his son, and that those officials at the Embassy in Abuja sent a cable to the National Counterterrorism Center. State Department officials maintain they had insufficient information to revoke his visa at that time.

Chapter 4 – Congress has broad plenary authority to determine classes of aliens who may be admitted into the United States and the grounds for which they may be removed. Pursuant to the Immigration and Nationality Act (INA), as amended, certain conduct may either disqualify an alien from entering the United States ("inadmissibility") or provide grounds for his or her removal/deportation. Prominently included among this conduct is criminal activity. "Criminal activity" comprises acts violative of federal, state, or, in many cases, foreign criminal law. It does *not* cover violations of the INA that are not crimes—most notably, being in the U.S. without legal permission. Thus, the term "illegal alien"—an alien without legal status—is not synonymous with "criminal alien."

Most crimes affecting immigration status are not specifically mentioned by the INA, but instead fall under a broad category of crimes, such as *crimes involving moral turpitude* or *aggravated felonies*. In addition, certain criminal conduct precludes a finding of *good moral character* under the INA, which is a requirement for naturalization and certain types of immigration relief.

In certain circumstances, grounds for inadmissibility or deportation may be waived. In some cases, aliens facing removal may be allowed to remain in the United States—for example, when they are granted discretionary or mandatory relief from removal for humanitarian reasons, such as through asylum, withholding of removal, or cancellation of removal. Aliens facing removal may also be permitted to depart the United States voluntarily, and thereby avoid the potential stigma and legal consequences of forced removal.

Criminal conduct may affect an alien's eligibility for either voluntary departure or discretionary relief from removal. Additionally, criminal conduct is a key disqualifying factor under the character requirement for naturalization.

Several legislative proposals were made during the 110th Congress that contained provisions modifying the immigration consequences of criminal activity. Enacted legislation modifying the immigration consequences of criminal activity included P.L. 110-257, providing certain relief from inadmissibility to members of the African National Congress; P.L. 110-340, making persons who have engaged in the recruitment of child soldiers in violation of federal law inadmissible, deportable and ineligible for asylum or withholding of removal; and P.L. 110-457, modifying the grounds for inadmissibility and removal related to human trafficking.

In: Removal and Exclusion of Foreign Nationals ISBN: 978-1-63482-610-5
Editor: Delia Gibson

Chapter 1

ALIEN REMOVALS AND RETURNS: OVERVIEW AND TRENDS*

Alison Siskin

SUMMARY

The ability to remove foreign nationals (aliens) who violate U.S. immigration law is central to the immigration enforcement system. Some lawful migrants violate the terms of their admittance, and some aliens enter the United States illegally, despite U.S. immigration laws and enforcement. In 2012, there were an estimated 11.4 million resident unauthorized aliens; estimates of other removable aliens, such as lawful permanent residents who commit crimes, are elusive. With total repatriations of over 600,000 people in FY2013—including about 440,000 formal removals—the removal and return of such aliens have become important policy issues for Congress, and key issues in recent debates about immigration reform.

The Immigration and Nationality Act (INA) provides broad authority to the Department of Homeland Security (DHS) and the Department of Justice (DOJ) to remove certain foreign nationals from the United States, including unauthorized aliens (i.e., foreign nationals who enter without inspection, aliens who enter with fraudulent documents, and aliens who enter legally but overstay the terms of their temporary visas) and lawfully

* This is an edited, reformatted and augmented version of a Congressional Research Service publication R43892, prepared for Members and Committees of Congress, dated February 3, 2015.

present foreign nationals who commit certain acts that make them removable. Any foreign national found to be inadmissible or deportable under the grounds specified in the INA may be ordered removed. The INA describes procedures for making and reviewing such a determination, and specifies conditions under which certain grounds of removal may be waived. DHS officials may exercise certain forms of discretion in pursuing removal orders, and certain removable aliens may be eligible for permanent or temporary relief from removal. Certain grounds for removal (e.g., criminal grounds, terrorist grounds) render foreign nationals ineligible for most forms of relief and may make them eligible for more streamlined (expedited) removal processes.

The "standard" removal process is a civil judicial proceeding in which an immigration judge from DOJ's Executive Office for Immigration Review (EOIR) determines whether an alien is removable. Immigration judges may grant certain forms of relief during the removal process (e.g., asylum, cancellation of removal), and the judge's removal decisions are subject to administrative and judicial review. The INA also describes different types of streamlined removal procedures, which generally include more-limited opportunities for relief and grounds for review. In addition, two alternative forms of removal exempt aliens from certain penalties associated with formal removal: voluntary departure (return) and withdrawal of petition for admission. These are often called "returns."

Following an order of removal, an alien is inadmissible for a minimum of five years after the date of the removal, and therefore is generally ineligible to return to the United States during this time period. The period of inadmissibility is determined by the reason for and type of removal. For example, a foreign national ordered removed based on removal proceedings initiated upon the foreign national's arrival is inadmissible for five years, while a foreign national ordered removed after being apprehended within the United States is inadmissible for 10 years. The length of inadmissibility increases to 20 years for an alien's second or subsequent removal order, and is indefinite for a foreign national convicted of an aggravated felony.

Absent additional factors, unlawful presence in the United States is a civil violation, not a criminal offense, and removal and its associated administrative processes are civil proceedings. As such, aliens in removal proceedings generally have no right to counsel (though they may be represented by counsel at their own expense). In addition, because removal is not considered punishment by the courts, Congress may impose immigration consequences retroactively.

There were a record number of removals between FY2009 and FY2013, including 438,421 removals in FY2013. Approximately 71% of the foreign nationals removed were from Mexico. However, during the same time period the number of returns (most of which occur at the

Southwest border) decreased to a low of 178,371 in FY2013—the fewest returns since 1968.

INTRODUCTION

Regardless of how a country regulates its immigration, some lawfully admitted foreign nationals may violate the conditions proscribed for being in the country, and some foreign nationals may enter the country illegally. Thus, in the United States, as in other countries, the removal of unauthorized aliens[1] and other aliens who violate the conditions under which they were admitted (e.g., overstaying their authorized period of stay, committing a crime while in the country) is central to immigration enforcement.

The removal and return of aliens to their country of nationality have become important policy issues for Congress, and tend to be key issues in debates about immigration reform. In 2012, there were an estimated 11.4 million resident unauthorized aliens in the United States;[2] estimates of other removable aliens, such as lawful permanent residents (LPRs)[3] who commit crimes, are elusive. More than 600,000 foreign nationals were repatriated from the United States in FY2013—including about 440,000 formal removals.[4]

The Immigration and Nationality Act (INA)[5] provides broad authority to the Department of Homeland Security (DHS) and the Department of Justice (DOJ) to remove certain aliens from the United States,[6] including unauthorized aliens and lawfully present foreign nationals who commit certain crimes. The different removal processes are spelled out in several sections of the INA,[7] which identifies two overarching reasons aliens may be removed from the United States: on the basis of *inadmissibility* or on the basis of *deportability* (see "Reasons for the Removal of a Foreign National"). The Illegal Immigration Reform and Immigrant Responsibility Act of 1996 (IIRIRA, P.L. 104-208), established new mechanisms by which to effectuate the removal of aliens who have violated the nation's immigration laws—including several streamlined processes. An alien's immigration status and whether the alien has engaged in certain specified activities (e.g., committed a particular criminal offense) determines which process is used. Lawful permanent residents are generally subject to the standard removal process where foreign nationals have their cases decided by an immigration judge. However, arriving aliens who have not been admitted into the country, as well as aliens within the United States who have committed specified criminal offenses, may be subject to more streamlined removal processes such as reinstatement of removal or expedited removal of criminal aliens.

This report provides an overview of the statutory framework for removal and briefly describes the standard removal process. It also describes several streamlined forms of removal, and two alternative forms of removal (often referred to as returns) that exempt aliens from certain penalties associated with formal removal: voluntary departure and withdrawal of petition for admission. In addition, the report discusses recent trends in removals and returns, and concludes with a summary of potential avenues for relief from removal.

This report does not provide any legal analysis on these topics and does not discuss court cases related to removal. It also does not discuss how removable foreign nationals are identified and located (e.g., the Criminal Alien Program), or how the government chooses which removable aliens to initiate removal proceedings against (i.e., prosecutorial discretion).

REASONS FOR THE REMOVAL OF A FOREIGN NATIONAL

The INA identifies two overarching reasons aliens may be removed from the United States: on the basis of *inadmissibility* or on the basis of *deportability*. Prior to the implementation of the IIRIRA, the INA included separate provisions governing the "exclusion" of aliens who were ineligible to enter the country (i.e., "excludable" persons) and the "deportation" of certain aliens within the United States (i.e., "deportable" persons).[8] The IIRIRA created a single proceeding to cover both types of removable aliens. Nonetheless, the INA retains two separate grounds for removal: (1) for aliens who have not been admitted to the United States and are inadmissible under INA §212,[9] and (2) for aliens who have been admitted to the United States (i.e., entered legally) and are deportable under INA §237(a).[10] Taken together the grounds of inadmissibility and deportability form the grounds for removal (i.e., the statutory reason that an alien may be removed from the United States). The grounds of inadmissibility and deportability are similar but not identical, as outlined below. Whether foreign nationals facing removal are subject to the grounds of inadmissibility or the grounds of deportability depends upon their immigration statuses.[11]

Any alien found to be inadmissible under INA §212 or deportable under INA §237 may be ordered removed. The INA describes procedures for making and reviewing such a determination, and specifies conditions under which some of these provisions may be waived.[12] DHS officials may exercise certain forms of discretion in pursuing removal orders,[13] and certain removable aliens may be eligible for permanent or temporary relief from removal.[14] Nonetheless, some grounds for removal[15] (e.g., criminal grounds, terrorist grounds) render aliens ineligible for most forms of relief and may make the alien eligible for a streamlined removal process (see "Streamlined Removal Processes").

Grounds of Inadmissibility

Section 212(a) of the INA specifies broad classes of inadmissible aliens,[16] including those who

- have a "communicable disease of public health significance,"[17]
- have committed certain criminal offenses,[18]
- are terrorists or national security concerns,[19]
- are likely at any time to become a public charge (i.e., become indigent),[20]
- are seeking to work without proper labor certification,[21]
- are attempting to enter illegally or have previously violated immigration law,[22]
- are ineligible for citizenship,[23] or
- have been removed previously or were unlawfully present in the United States.[24]

Generally, the grounds of inadmissibility are applied to foreign nationals found in the country who have not been admitted (e.g., those who entered illegally/without inspection). In addition, certain streamlined removal processes (such as expedited removal) can only be applied to aliens who have not been admitted to the United States.

Grounds of Deportability

In order for a lawfully admitted alien to be ordered removed, the government has to prove that the noncitizen has violated a ground of deportation (e.g., overstaying his or her term of admittance).[25] The INA §237(a) specifies six broad classes of deportable aliens, including those who

- are inadmissible at time of entry or violate their immigration status;[26]
- commit certain criminal offenses,[27] including crimes of moral turpitude,[28] aggravated felonies,[29] alien smuggling, and high-speed flight from an immigration checkpoint;
- fail to register (if required under law) or commit document fraud;[30]
- are security risks (including aliens who violate any law relating to espionage, engage in criminal activity that endangers public safety, partake in terrorist activities, or assisted in Nazi persecution or genocide);[31]
- become a public charge within five years of entry;[32] or
- vote unlawfully.[33]

Consequences of an Order of Removal

INA §241 describes the general consequences of an order of removal, including what must occur after one has been issued. Aliens under a final order of removal normally are required to depart the United States within 90 days and may be detained until the removal order is executed. Usually, the Secretary of DHS must remove an alien within 90 days of the alien receiving a final order of removal (also see "Removal Process"). Under most circumstances, INA §241 requires that aliens under a final order of removal be detained until the removal order is executed (i.e., until the alien is removed from the country).[34] In addition, aliens who are not detained and cannot be removed within 90 days face other supervision requirements.[35]

Following an order of removal, an alien is inadmissible to the United States for a minimum of five years after the date of the removal, and therefore is generally ineligible during the period of inadmissibility to return to the United States in the absence of an applicable exception. The period of inadmissibility is determined by the reason for the removal and the type of removal process used. For example, an alien who is ordered removed based on removal proceedings initiated upon the alien's arrival is inadmissible for five years, while an alien ordered removed after being apprehended within the United States is inadmissible for 10 years.[36] The length of inadmissibility increases to 20 years in the case of an alien's second or subsequent removal order, and is indefinite in the case of an alien convicted of an aggravated felony.[37]

Removal Processes

Absent additional factors, unlawful presence in the United States is a civil violation, not a criminal offense,[38] and removal and its associated administrative processes are civil proceedings.[39] Thus, aliens in removal proceedings generally have no right to appointed counsel (though they may be represented by counsel at their own expense).[40] In addition, Congress may pass legislation that imposes immigration consequences retroactively.[41]

Certain DHS personnel may initiate a removal process against an alien by presenting the alien with a notice to appear (NTA).[42] The NTA outlines the INA provisions that the alien is charged with violating (i.e., one of the grounds of inadmissibility or deportability discussed in "Reasons for the Removal of a Foreign National").

Upon the receipt of an NTA, foreign nationals may be detained during removal proceedings, and certain foreign nationals are subject to mandatory detention.[43] Foreign nationals who are not subject to mandatory detention may be released on bond or their own recognizance. An alien who is eligible to be released on bond may request a bond redetermination hearing before an immigration judge to have the bond lowered, or to be given bond if it was denied by DHS. During the bond hearing, the alien must prove that he or she is not a flight risk or a danger to society.[44] Bond hearings are not considered part of the removal process.

The standard removal process under INA §240 is a trial-like proceeding in which an attorney from DHS presents the government's case for why the alien should be removed and an immigration judge from the Department of Justice's Executive Office for Immigration Review (EOIR) determines whether the alien should be removed. The standard removal process is only one of several ways aliens may be removed from the United States. An alien may concede removability (i.e., accept stipulated removal) rather than undergoing the standard removal proceeding. In addition, an alien may be subject to one of several types of streamlined removal procedures, which generally include more-limited opportunities for relief and review than the standard removal process (see "Streamlined Removal Processes").[45]

Standard Removal Process (INA §240)

The standard removal process is a civil administrative proceeding in which an EOIR immigration judge determines whether an alien is removable. Immigration judges may grant certain forms of relief (see "Relief from Removal") during the removal proceeding, and their removal decisions are subject to certain forms of review.

Apart from a possible bond hearing related to detention, generally an alien first appears in immigration court at a preliminary hearing. An alien who fails to appear for a removal hearing (absent exceptional circumstances) can be removed *in absentia* and becomes inadmissible for five years,[46] as well as ineligible for relief from removal for 10 years.[47] Some cases—such as i*n absentia* cases, cases where the respondent concedes removability, and cases where both the government and the alien agree to the relief—can be decided at the preliminary hearing stage. Otherwise, a time may be set for an individual merits hearing.

During the individual merits hearing, the government's attorney attempts to prove the charges on the NTA. The government and the alien can present witnesses, and the judge rules on whether the foreign national is removable from the United States and is eligible for relief from removal if requested by the foreign national.[48] Generally, within 30 days after the decision, the government's attorney or the foreign national may appeal the decision to the Board of Immigration Appeals (BIA).[49] After the BIA decision, the alien may appeal to a federal court.[50]

Stipulated Removal (INA §240(d))

INA §240(d) allows for an immigration judge to enter a removal order for an alien who concedes removability without the alien undergoing a standard removal proceeding in front of an immigration judge. The foreign national must fill out a detailed form, which must be approved by DHS. Generally, only those who have no possibility of relief from removal accept stipulated removal. A stipulated removal order generally has the same repercussions as a removal order issued at the end of an immigration proceeding in terms of triggering the grounds of inadmissibility.

Streamlined Removal Processes

In 1996, Congress amended the INA to establish several streamlined removal procedures though which an alien could be removed with limited or no review by the immigration courts.[51] These removal procedures tend to limit the types of relief available (see "Relief from Removal") and judicial review, compared to hearings under the standard removal process. In recent years, these streamlined removal processes have accounted for a higher percentage of total removals than standard removals, and are responsible for most of the growth in the overall number of removals (see *Figure 3*).

Expedited Removal of Arriving Aliens (INA §235(b))[52]

Under expedited removal (INA §235(b)), an alien who lacks proper documentation or has committed fraud or willful misrepresentation of facts to gain admission into the United States is inadmissible and may be removed without any further hearings or review,[53] unless the alien indicates an intention to apply for asylum or another form of removal based on a fear of persecution.[54] Aliens from Western Hemisphere countries with which the United States does not have full diplomatic relations (e.g., Cuba) are excluded from expedited removal.[55] In addition, under policy, unaccompanied minors[56] are placed in expedited removal in very limited circumstances.[57]

Aliens subject to expedited removal must be detained until they are removed and may only be released due to a medical emergency or, if necessary, for law enforcement purposes.[58] Although under law the Secretary of Homeland Security[59] may apply expedited removal to any alien who has not been admitted or paroled[60] into the United States and who cannot show that he or she has been continuously present for two years, expedited removal has only been applied to aliens

- arriving at ports of entry;
- arriving by sea who are not admitted or paroled; and
- who are present in the United States without being admitted or paroled, are encountered by an immigration officer within 100 air miles of the U.S. international land border, and have not established to the satisfaction of an immigration officer that they have been physically present in the United States continuously for the 14-day period immediately preceding the date of encounter.

The INA provides immigration protections to aliens who have a well-founded fear of persecution, most notably in the form of asylum status. Aliens who are in expedited removal and request asylum are given a "credible fear" hearing to determine if there is support for their asylum claim.[61] Those who pass the credible fear hearing are placed into standard removal proceedings under INA §240. In addition, aliens who receive negative "credible fear" determinations may request that an immigration judge review the case. Aliens who have been subject to expedited removal are barred from reentering the United States for at least five years.[62]

Expedited Removal of Aliens Convicted of Aggravated Felonies (INA §238)

Aliens who have been convicted of certain crimes are barred from most types of relief from removal,[63] and, partially as a result of this, the INA contains provisions to accelerate the removal of noncitizens who have been convicted of such crimes.[64] Generally, those who are removable because of a criminal act are subject to mandatory detention while awaiting removal.[65] Aliens removed on criminal grounds are generally subject to bars on reentering the United States ranging from 10 years to indefinite, depending on the nature of the offense committed and whether they had been removed previously.[66]

INA §238(a)(1) allows for removal proceedings for aliens convicted of certain crimes to be conducted at federal, state, and local correctional facilities. The goal of this provision is to be able to expeditiously remove the alien when the alien has completed his criminal sentence, and limit the amount of time that an alien must remain in DHS custody pending removal.[67]

In addition, INA §238(b) authorizes the government to determine that certain noncitizens are deportable without having the decision on removability made by an immigration judge.[68] To be eligible for removal under INA §238(b), an alien cannot be an LPR and must have been convicted of an aggravated felony.[69] Although the alien is not entitled to a hearing before an immigration judge, the alien is entitled to

- "reasonable" notice of the charges and an opportunity to inspect the evidence and rebut the charges;
- counsel, at no expense to the government;
- a determination that the foreign national is in fact the person named in the notice; and
- a record of the proceedings for judicial review.[70]

Because foreign nationals removed under this provision have been convicted of at least one aggravated felony, they are indefinitely barred from reentering the United States.[71]

Reinstatement of Removal (INA §241(a)(5))

Another streamlined removal process is for the government to reinstate a previously issued removal order. A foreign national who is found to have reentered the United States illegally after being removed or leaving under voluntary departure (see "Voluntary Departure (INA §240B)") can have their prior removal order reinstated by DHS. The reinstatement order is not subject to review by an immigration judge and the foreign national is ineligible for all types of relief from removal with the exception of withholding of removal[72] and a claim based on the Convention Against Torture (see "Temporary Types of Relief from Removal").[73] A person who was ordered removed but reentered the country legally is not subject to reinstatement of removal.[74]

ALTERNATIVE FORMS OF REMOVAL (I.E., RETURNS)

Until FY2013, the majority of aliens apprehended along the Southwest border were not subject to the standard removal procedures or expedited removal (see "Statistics on Removals and Returns"); instead, the majority of these aliens were allowed to either undergo voluntary departure or withdraw their applications. Voluntary departure and withdraw of application are often referred to as types of *returns* rather than removals. In addition, some aliens within the country accept voluntary departure either as an alternative to having a judge render a decision regarding their removability or at the conclusion of their removal proceeding.

Voluntary Departure (INA §240B)

Some consider voluntary departure a type of relief from removal because it does not carry the same consequences (i.e., the same time bars for reentering the country or criminal consequences for those who reenter) as other types of removal. Nonetheless, unlike those who receive other types of relief from removal, aliens who are granted voluntary departure are not permitted to remain in the United States for an extended period of time.[75]

The INA authorizes voluntary departure at two distinct times—before the conclusion of removal proceedings and at the conclusion of removal proceedings—with different requirements and restrictions.[76] However, regulations implementing voluntary departure created three periods for seeking voluntary departure and established conditions for voluntary departure at each juncture. The periods are (1) before the initiation of removal proceedings, (2) after the initiation of removal proceedings but before the proceedings are concluded, and (3) at the conclusion of removal proceedings.[77] An alien must request voluntary departure in order to receive it.[78] Aliens who are removable because of a conviction for an aggravated felony or on terrorist grounds are ineligible for voluntary departure. Those who were granted voluntary departure but failed to depart within the specified time are ineligible for 10 years for voluntary departure and most types of relief from removal.[79]

At the border, voluntary departure is available only to aliens from contiguous territories (i.e., Canada and Mexico), and aliens are escorted to the point of departure.[80] DHS Customs and Border Patrol (CBP) inspectors can also permit aliens traveling through a point of entry (POE) to withdraw their applications for admission and return to their points of origin. Voluntary departure costs less than most types of removal procedures since, in most cases, the government does not have to pay for the foreign nationals' return to their home countries.

Withdraw of Application (INA §235(a)(4))

At the discretion of the government, an applicant for admission to the United States may be permitted to withdraw his or her application and depart immediately from the United States without being subject to the five-year bar on reentry.[81] An alien may be permitted to withdraw the application if it is determined that it is in the best interest of justice that a removal (or expedited removal) order not be issued, and that the alien has both the intent and means to depart immediately from the United States.[82] The alien's decision to withdraw the application must be made voluntarily. In general, an alien who has withdrawn an application for admission must be detained, either by DHS or the owner of the vessel (e.g., airline) on which he or she arrived, until departure.[83]

STATISTICS ON REMOVALS AND RETURNS

There are two sets of statistics regarding removals and returns of aliens from the United States. The first set is from DHS' Office of Immigration Statistics (OIS) and include removals and returns by both Immigration and Customs Enforcement (ICE) in the interior of the country and by CBP at the borders. Additionally, ICE produces its own statistics on removals that do not include CBP's statistics. CRS presents both sets of data because different information can be obtained from the manner in which each maintains and presents its data. For example, ICE is able to provide data on the grounds (i.e., main reason) for removal, which is not captured in data from OIS.

Overall, both sets of data present a similar picture of removals. The data show an increase in the total number of removals, driven mostly by an increase in the use of expedited removal processes and a decrease in the use of returns (i.e., voluntary departure and withdraw of application). The decrease in returns is most likely attributable to a policy change that places more aliens in removal processes rather than allowing them to withdraw their applications, and to a decrease in the total number of apprehensions along the Southwest border.[84]

Aliens Removed and Returned Since 1995

In FY1995 the number of removals was significantly less than the number of returns, but since FY2011 the number of removals has outpaced the number of returns. In FY1995 there were just 50,924 removals compared to over 1.3 million returns. Between FY1996 and FY1998 the number of removals increased 151%, from 69,680 to 174,813, corresponding to changes made in IIRIRA[85] that expanded the grounds for removal and tightened the standards for relief from removal. In addition, the changes made to the grounds for removal (i.e., the statutory reasons a foreign national can be removed) were retroactive. For example, some aliens had committed crimes prior to 1996 that were not removable offenses at the time, but the changes made in 1996 made these aliens removable. Although the number of returns remained relatively constant between FY1996 and FY1998 (about 1.5 million a year), and the number of removals more than doubled during the same period, the number of returns remained significantly higher than the number of removals.

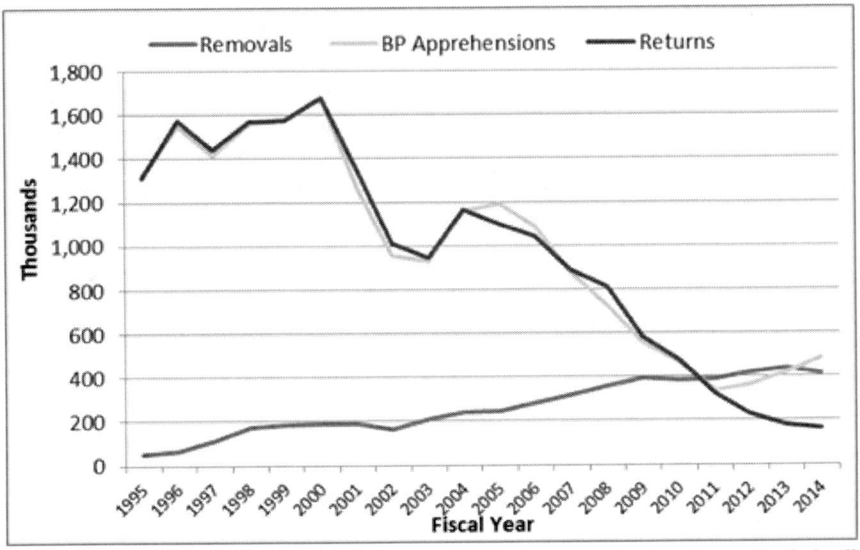

Source: Department of Homeland Security, "DHS Released End of Year Statistics," press release, December 19, 2014. Department of Homeland Security, Office of Immigration Statistics, Yearbook of Immigration Statistics: 2013, Washington, DC, Tables 35, 39; http://www.dhs.gov/yearbook-immigration-statistics-2013-enforcement-actions. Department of Justice, Immigration and Naturalization Service, Yearbook of Immigration Statistics: 2001, Washington, DC, February 2003, p. 233.

Figure 1. Removals, Returns, and Border Patrol (BP) Apprehensions. (FY1995-FY2014).

With the exception of one year (FY2002), the number of removals increased between FY1997 and FY2009. The number of removals remained relatively stable between FY2009 and FY2011, and then increased again between FY2011 and FY2013. The number of removals declined between FY2013 and FY2014. Some of the overall growth in removals since FY2002 may be related to enforcement efforts in response to the terrorist attacks of September 11, 2001.[86] In addition, funding for immigration enforcement increased during this period.[87] The highest number of removals occurred in FY2013 (438,421).

In contrast, the number of returns has fluctuated over the past 25 years, and is at its lowest level since the late 1960s.[88] Because returns are mostly of Mexican nationals who have been apprehended by the Border Patrol, they are closely tied with border patrol apprehensions (*Figure 1*).[89] The divergence between the number of returns and border patrol apprehensions since FY2012 may be partially attributable to the rise in the number of apprehensions of persons from countries other than Mexico. For example, foreign nationals from countries other than Mexico accounted for 47% of all border patrol apprehensions in FY2013, compared to 13% in FY2010.[90] Another factor may be CBP's effort in recent years to promote "high consequence" enforcement for unauthorized Mexicans apprehended at the border (this is known as the Consequence Delivery System). Historically, immigration agents permitted most Mexicans apprehended at the border to voluntarily return to Mexico without any penalty. Since 2005, CBP has limited voluntary returns in favor of formal removals (e.g., standard removal proceedings, expedited removal) and criminal changes (e.g., for illegal entry or re-entry after deportation).[91]

With the exception of FY2003, the number of returns exceeded 1 million persons a year between FY1997 and FY2006. Since FY2004 the number of returns has steadily decreased to a low of 162,814 in FY2014. Notably, FY2011 was the first year since FY1941 that the number of returns was less than the number of removals.

Removal Statistics Since FY2002

With certain exceptions, a removal proceeding under INA §240 is, according to the statute, the "exclusive procedure" for determining whether an alien should be removed from the United States. However, as discussed in this section, there has been a recent trend toward using expedited procedures.

OIS data show that the number of removals more than doubled between FY2002 and FY2009, from 165,168 to 393,457. The number of removals then decreased by approximately 8,000 between FY2009 and FY2010, and then increased more than 30,000 between FY2010 and FY2012. According to OIS, the highest number of removals occurred in FY2013.

As *Table 1* shows, statistics provided by ICE present a slightly different picture. According to ICE data, total removals increased more than threefold between FY2002 and FY2012, from 122,587 to 409,849, and then decreased in FY2013 and FY2014. The largest proportional increases in removals occurred between FY2005 and FY2008. Removals increased 15% between FY2005 and FY2006, 40% between FY2006 and FY2007, and 27% between FY2007 and FY2008. Between FY2012 and FY2014, the number of removals decreased 23%, to the lowest level since FY2007.

Table 1. Total Number of Removals: OIS and ICE FY2002-FY2014

Fiscal Year	OIS	ICE
2002	165,168	122,587
2003	211,098	157,080
2004	240,665	175,106
2005	246,431	180,18
2006	280,974	207,77
2007	319,382	291,06
2008	359,795	369,22
2009	391,932	389,83
2010	383,031	392,86
2011	387,134	396,90
2012	418,397	409,84
2013	438,421	368,64
2014	414,481	315,94

Source: Department of Homeland Security, "DHS Released End of Year Statistics," press release, December 19, 2014. Department of Homeland Security, Office of Immigration Statistics, Yearbook of Immigration Statistics: 2013, Washington, DC, Table 39; http://www.dhs.gov/yearbook-immigration-statistics-2013-enforcement-actions; Immigration and Customs Enforcement, FY 2013 ICE Immigration Removals, ERO Annual Report, Washington, DC, http://www.ice.gov/doclib/about/offices/ero/pdf/2013-ice-immigration-removals.pdf; and unpublished data provided to CRS by ICE.

Note: ICE removals include voluntary departures (INA §240B) while OIS removals do not.

Interestingly, ICE appears to have accounted for the overwhelming majority of all DHS' removals between FY2007 and FY2012; this was not the case between FY2002 and FY2006 or in FY2013 and FY2014. In other words, the growth in removals between FY2002 and FY2006 and between FY2012 and FY2013 was driven by removals of those aliens apprehended at or between ports of entry. The decline in removals between FY2013 and FY2014 was solely a result of the decline in those removed by ICE.

Removals by Type

OIS and ICE data show similar trends regarding the increasing use of more streamlined removal processes and the decrease in the number of removals processed by the immigration courts.

OIS Data

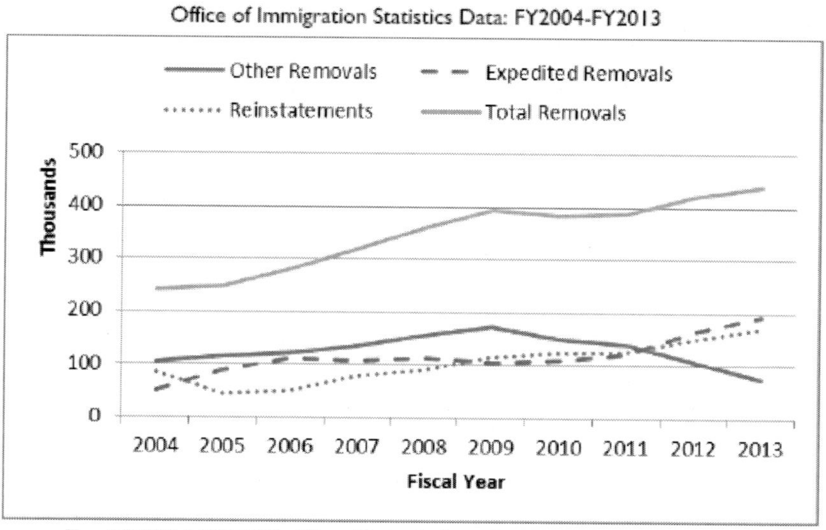

Source: For FY2004-FY2009: Unpublished data from DHS Office of Immigration Statistics; for FY2010: John F. Simanski and Lesley M. Sapp, Immigration Enforcement Actions: 2012, Department of Homeland Security, Office of Immigration Statistics, Washington, DC, December 2013, p. 5; for FY2011-FY2013: John F. Simanski, Immigration Enforcement Actions: 2013, Department of Homeland Security, Office of Immigration Statistics, Washington, DC, September 2014, p. 5.

Note: Other removals include standard removals (INA §240), expedited removals of criminal aliens (INA §238), and voluntary departures (INA §240B). Expedited removals only include removals under INA §235(b). Data for FY2014 were not available at time of publication.

Figure 2. Removals by Type.

As shown in *Figure 2*, the numbers of all types of removals increased between FY2004 and FY2013. The numbers of expedited removals of arriving aliens and reinstatements have increased significantly since FY2004, reaching their highest levels in FY2013. There were 193,032 expedited removals and 170,247 reinstatements in FY2013. Since FY2004, the number of aliens subject to expedited removal increased approximately threefold and the number of reinstatements of removal orders more than doubled. The number of standard removals, voluntary departures, and expedited removals of criminal aliens ("other removals") increased between FY2004 and FY2011, and then decreased in FY2012 and FY2013. Thus, since FY2010 the increase in the total number of removals has been driven exclusively by the increases in expedited removals of arriving aliens and reinstatements.

Office of Immigration Statistics Data: FY2004-FY2013

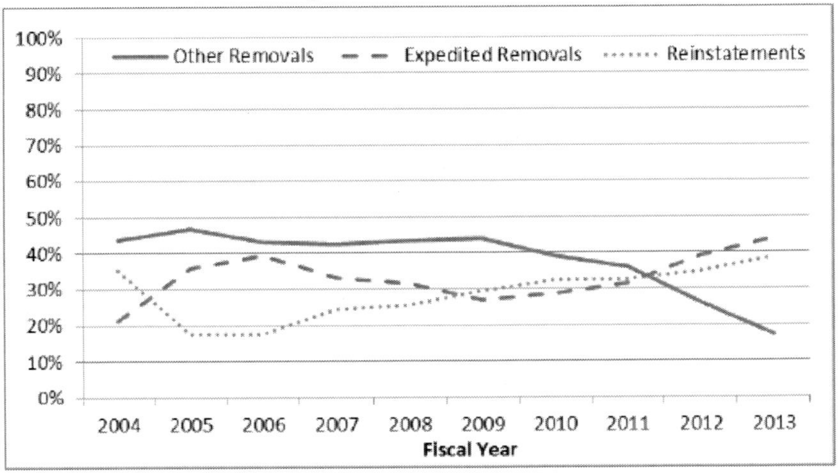

Source: For FY2004-FY2009: Unpublished data from DHS Office of Immigration Statistics; for FY2010: John F. Simanski and Lesley M. Sapp, Immigration Enforcement Actions: 2012, Department of Homeland Security, Office of Immigration Statistics, Washington, DC, December 2013, p. 5; for FY2011-FY2013: John F. Simanski, Immigration Enforcement Actions: 2013, Department of Homeland Security, Office of Immigration Statistics, Washington, DC, September 2014, p. 5.

Note: Other removals include standard removals (INA §240), expedited removals of criminal (INA §238) and voluntary departures (INA §240B). Expedited removals only includes removals under INA §235(b). Reinstatements of removal are under INA §241(a)(5). Data for FY2014 were not available at time of publication.

Figure 3. Removals by Type, as a Percentage of Total Removals.

Standard removals, voluntary departures, and expedited removals of criminal aliens ("other removals") accounted for 17% of all removals in

FY2013, while expedited removals comprised 44% of those removed and reinstatements accounted for almost 39% of all removals (see *Figure 3*). Comparatively, approximately 44% of all removals were other removals in FY2004; since then these types of removals have comprised a smaller and shrinking proportion of the removed population. Expedited removals accounted for approximately 21% of those removed in FY2004, but 35.7% of all removals in FY2005. The increase in the proportion (and overall numbers) of expedited removals at that time may be attributable to the expansion of the categories of aliens subject to expedited removal.92 Reinstatements declined as a percentage of removals between FY2004 and FY2005, and then steadily increased. Thus, as discussed, the increase in removals during the past decade has been driven by an increase in the use of expedited removals and reinstatements of removal orders.

ICE Data

The data from ICE are presented differently than those from OIS simply by way of how the entities maintain their data. In addition, OIS statistics include those apprehended at and between ports of entry (i.e., those apprehended by CBP) while ICE provides data on removals and returns of those apprehended in the interior of the country by that agency.

As shown in *Figure 4*, more than 90% of those repatriated in FY2013 were subject to removal, while approximately 10% were classified as returns. Of the 332,538 aliens formally removed (i.e., not given voluntary departure or allowed to withdraw their application) by ICE in that year, 35% (115,940) were removed under the INA grounds of deportability and 65% (216,598) were removed under the INA grounds of inadmissibility.[93]

Returns (e.g., voluntary departure, voluntary return witnessed by ICE), as both a percentage of all removals (i.e., removals and formal returns together) and an absolute number, decreased between FY2008 and FY2012. Notably, the overall decrease in removals between FY2012 and FY2013 was driven by a decrease in the number of returns (see *Figure 4*).[94]

In addition, of the aliens formally removed (as opposed to returned) since FY2008, the overwhelming majority have been removed under the grounds of inadmissibility rather than the grounds of deportability. Nonetheless, there has been an increase in the proportion of those removed under the grounds of deportability over the six years, from 21% in FY2008 to 35% in FY2013.

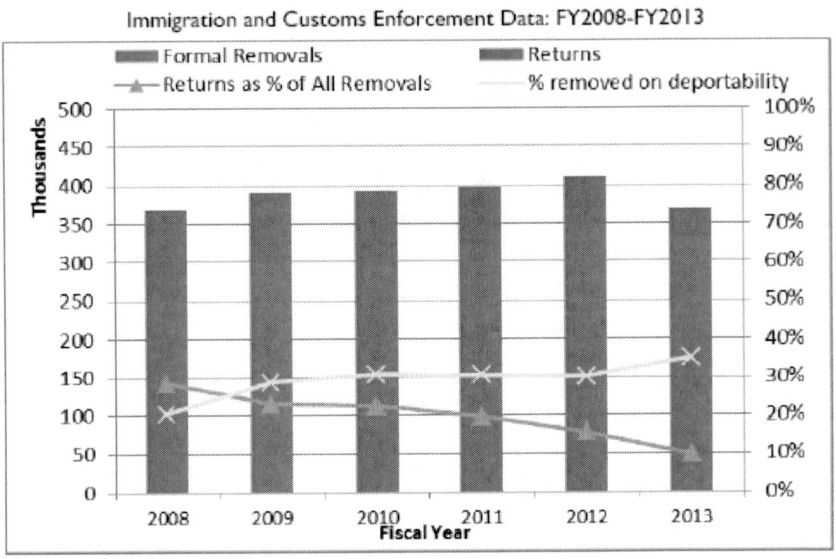

Source: CRS analysis of unpublished data from DHS Immigration and Customs Enforcement (ICE).

Note: Data for FY2014 were not available at time of publication.

Figure 4. All Removals: Formal Removals and Returns.

Removals by Country

Over the 10-year period from FY2004 through FY2013, the majority of removals were of Mexican nationals (70.5%) (see *Figure 5* and *Table A-1*). In FY2013, four countries accounted for approximately 96% of all removals: Mexico (71.8%), Guatemala (10.7%), Honduras (8.3%), and El Salvador (4.8%). No other country represented more than 1% of all removals in FY2013.

Over the 10-year period there was a significant increase in the number of people removed to those countries. The number of people removed from El Salvador more than doubled over the 10-year period, while the number of people removed from Honduras more than tripled, and the number of people removed from Guatemala increased more than four-fold. (See *Table A-1*.) The number of those removed from Mexico increased by 79%, much less of a percentage increase than for the three Central American countries.

FY2004-FY2013

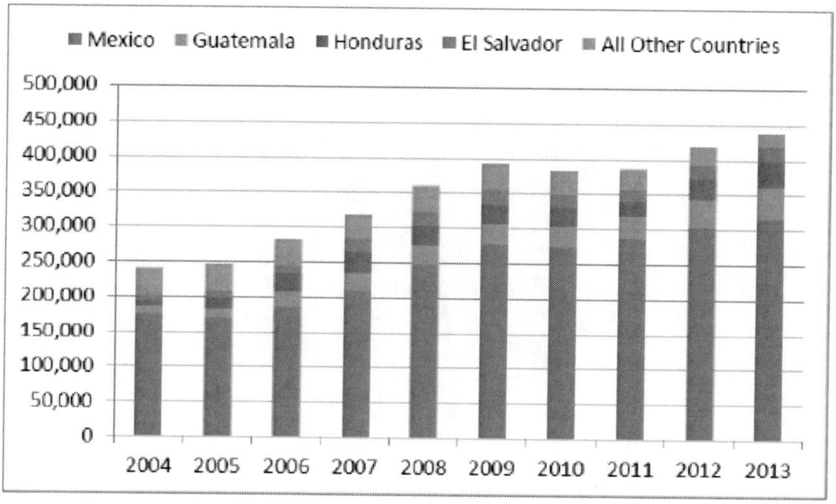

Source: Department of Homeland Security, Office of Immigration Statistics, Yearbook of Immigration Statistics: 2013, Washington, DC, Table 41.

Notes: For the numbers and percentages, see Table A-1. Data for FY2014 were not available at time of publication.

Figure 5. Removals by Coutry.

Outcomes of Immigration Proceedings

In an immigration proceeding, an immigration judge must decide as part of the standard removal process whether the charges against an alien should be sustained. If the charges are not sustained or the alien establishes eligibility for naturalization, the judge terminates the case. If the charges are sustained, the judge determines whether to order the alien removed, grant voluntary departure,[95] or grant relief (discussed in the next section).[96] In addition, there are some cases that are completed without the immigration judge rendering a decision. Most of these cases are administrative closures.[97] As *Figure 6* shows, in FY2013 the majority of completed cases resulted in removals (voluntary departures are included in removals), while 18% of the completions were other (mostly administrative) closures. In addition, approximately 13% of the decisions were terminations, and 15% were grants of relief.

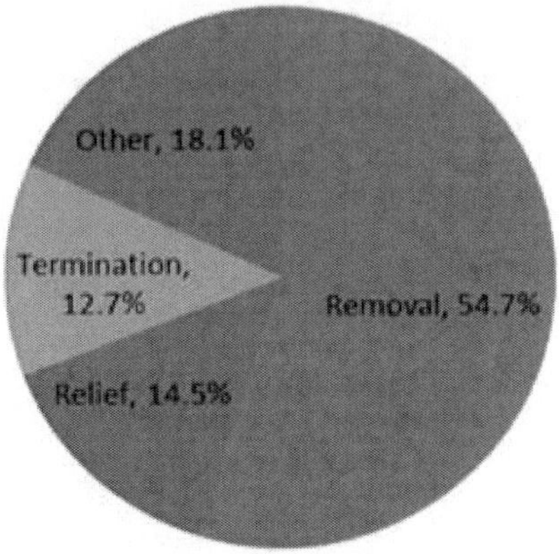

Source: CRS analysis of data from the U.S. Department of Justice, Executive Office for Immigration Review, FY2013 Statistical Year Book, Falls Church, VA, April 2014, pp. D2-D5.

Note: Total number of completions was 192,065. Voluntary departures are counted as removals. The "other" category includes administrative closures, transfers, changes of venues, failure of prosecute, Temporary Protected Status (TPS), and other administrative completions. Over 93% of the other category is administrative closures.

Figure 6. Outcomes of Completed Cases: FY2013.

RELIEF FROM REMOVAL

There are mechanisms under the INA that allow certain removable aliens to remain in the United States, either permanently or temporarily. This section provides an overview of the types of relief from removal available under the INA. It begins with a discussion of the types of relief that confer or can lead to lawful permanent resident (LPR) status for an alien. The discussion then shifts to types of relief from removal that allow aliens to remain in the United States but do not confer an immigration status that would allow them to remain in the country permanently. Aliens in removal proceedings may apply for more than one type of relief.[98]

Among the proceedings initially decided by an immigration judge in FY2013, 40% of aliens had applications for some type of relief from removal.[99]

Permanent Relief from Removal

Some types of relief from removal allow an alien to adjust to LPR status either immediately or at a later time. LPRs, also known as immigrants, are foreign nationals who come to live permanently in the United States.

Cancellation of Removal

Cancellation of removal confers LPR status on certain removable noncitizens who have substantial ties to the United States or are of humanitarian concern (i.e., battered aliens).[100] In general, an alien applying for cancellation of removal must have substantial ties to the United States, be of good moral character, and not have been convicted of a crime that makes him or her removable. Requirements differ for aliens who are LPRs and aliens who are nonimmigrants or unauthorized aliens.[101] For example, nonimmigrants or unauthorized aliens have to demonstrate that their removal would cause extreme and unusual hardship to their families in the United States. This requirement does not apply to LPRs.[102] (For a discussion of the different types of cancellation of removal, see *Appendix B*.) In addition, the criminal offenses that make an alien ineligible for cancellation of removal are generally broader for nonpermanent residents than for permanent residents.

Applications for cancellation of removal can only be made in removal proceedings, and decisions to grant relief are made on a case-by-case basis. Because cancellation of removal is a discretionary form of relief (i.e., it is granted at the discretion of an immigration judge), there is no fixed standard of who merits relief. The burden is on the alien to show that he or she is eligible for and deserves the relief.[103] With few exceptions, grants of cancellation of removal are limited to 4,000 LPRs and 4,000 nonpermanent residents each fiscal year.[104] There were 3,542 LPRs and 3,922 non-LPRs who received cancellation of removal in FY2013.[105]

Defensive Asylum[106]

Foreign nationals seeking asylum must demonstrate a well-founded fear that if they were returned home they would be persecuted based upon one of five characteristics: race, religion, nationality, membership in a particular social group, or political opinion.[107]

Foreign nationals arriving or present in the United States may apply for asylum with U.S. Citizenship and Immigration Services (USCIS) after arrival into the country (affirmative claims), or they may seek asylum before an immigration judge during removal proceedings (defensive claims).

This section focuses on defensive claims for asylum since those only occur once someone is placed into removal proceedings.

Defensive applications for asylum are raised when a foreign national in removal proceedings asserts a claim for asylum as a defense to his or her removal. Generally, the alien raises the issue of asylum at the beginning of the removal process. Aliens who are granted asylum may apply for LPR status after one year.

Foreign nationals who participated in the persecution of other people are excluded from receiving asylum. The INA outlines other conditions for mandatory denials of asylum claims, including the following cases: the alien has been convicted of a serious crime and is a danger to the community; there are reasons for believing that the alien has committed a serious nonpolitical crime outside the United States; the alien has been firmly resettled in another country; or "there are reasonable grounds for regarding the alien as a danger to the security of the United States."[108] Under statute, an alien who has been convicted of an aggravated felony is considered to have been convicted of a serious crime.

There were 21,717 foreign nationals who requested asylum before an immigration judge during removal proceedings in FY2013. During the same year, immigration judges rendered decisions in 8,833 removal cases where a foreign national requested asylum, and the judges granted asylum in 30% of those cases.[109]

Adjustment to LPR Status

Adjustment of status is another type of permanent relief from removal. This is the process of becoming an LPR in the United States without having to go abroad to apply for a visa.[110]

At their discretion, immigration judges may adjust the status of a non-lawful permanent resident alien if certain requirements are met: (1) the alien is the beneficiary of an approved visa petition for LPR status based on family or employment ties; (2) an immigrant visa is immediately available; and (3) the alien is not otherwise inadmissible. There were 3,868 foreign nationals in immigration proceedings who received adjustment of status in FY2013.[111]

Temporary Types of Relief from Removal

Several types of relief from removal permit an alien to remain in the United States for a temporary, but unspecified, period of time. These types of relief are generally given to foreign nationals until conditions in their home countries change so that it is safe for them to return.

Withholding of Removal

Withholding of removal is closely related to, but different from, asylum.[112]

The INA prevents the U.S. government from removing an alien to a country where the government has determined that the alien's life would be threatened because of his or her race, religion, nationality, membership in a particular social group, or political opinion.[113] Whereas asylum is a discretionary form of relief, an immigration judge must grant withholding if the alien meets the requirements.[114] Under INA §241(b)(3) an applicant for asylum is also an applicant for withholding of removal.[115] An alien is ineligible for withholding of removal if

- the alien ordered, incited, assisted, or otherwise participated in the persecution of another individual;
- the alien was convicted of a particularly serious crime and is a danger to the community;[116]
- there is serious reason to believe that the alien committed a serious nonpolitical crime before arriving in the United States; or
- there are reasonable grounds to believe that the alien presents a security risk to the United States.

Unlike asylum, withholding of removal is not a pathway to LPR status, as the relief is temporary.[117] Foreign nationals granted withholding of removal may be removed to a third country provided that the country will allow their entry.[118]

There were 1,518 grants and 9,983 denials of withholding of removal (i.e., a 13% grant rate) in FY2013.[119]

Convention Against Torture

The United States is a party to the United Nations Convention Against Torture and Other Cruel, Inhuman, or Degrading Treatment or Punishment (CAT).[120] CAT Article 3 requires that no State Party shall expel, return, or extradite a person to another country where "there are substantial grounds for believing that he would be in danger of being subjected to torture." The regulations implementing CAT prohibit the removal of aliens to countries where they would more likely than not be subjected to torture.[121]

If country conditions change and the U.S. government believes the foreign national would no longer face torture in the country, the foreign national can be removed. Although some categories of foreign nationals are generally ineligible to receive asylum or withholding of removal (e.g., those aliens removable on security-related grounds or who have been convicted of certain criminal offenses), CAT protections prevent the removal of *any* foreign national to a country where he or she would be more likely than not to face torture.[122] Of the cases where a decision on the aliens' applications for CAT protections was made by an immigration judge, CAT was granted in 506 cases and denied in 9,575 cases.[123]

Temporary Protected Status[124]

Temporary Protected Status (TPS) is blanket relief that may be granted, provided that doing so is consistent with U.S. national interests, under the following conditions: there is ongoing armed conflict posing serious threat to personal safety; a foreign state requests TPS because it temporarily cannot handle the return of nationals due to environmental disaster; or there are extraordinary and temporary conditions in a foreign state that prevent aliens from returning.[125]

The Secretary of Homeland Security can issue TPS for periods of 6 to 18 months and can extend these periods if conditions do not change in the designated country.[126] To receive TPS, eligible foreign nationals must register with USCIS. TPS is not an immigration status, and aliens who receive TPS are not on an immigration track that leads to LPR status.[127] As of December 2014, 11 countries have TPS.[128]

Deferred Enforced Departure

Deferred Enforced Departure (DED) does not confer an immigration status. The granting of DED is not based upon any specific statutory authority, but instead is typically premised upon the Executive Branch's independent constitutional authority.[129] The discretionary procedures of DED are used to provide relief the Administration feels is appropriate by balancing judgments regarding foreign policy, humanitarian, and immigration concerns. Aliens covered by DED are usually not subject to removal from the United States for a designated period of time. Unlike TPS, aliens do not register with USCIS, but receive DED when they are in removal proceedings. The President sets the parameters of DED. For example, the President may authorize that aliens with DED receive work authorization. Only Liberians currently have DED, which is set to expire on September 30, 2016.[130]

Deferred Action

Deferred action is not an immigration status nor does it have a statutory authority; it is a form of administrative discretion.[131] DHS may decline to institute removal proceedings, terminate proceedings, or decline to execute a final order of removal. Approval of deferred action means that no action will be taken (for a specified time or indefinitely) against an apparently removable alien.[132]

For example, under an initiative known as Deferred Action for Childhood Arrivals (DACA) certain individuals without a lawful immigration status who were brought to the United States as children and meet other criteria may be granted deferred action for two years, subject to renewal.[133]

CONCLUSION

The Immigration and Nationality Act contains several different processes to effectuate the removal of aliens, as well as mechanisms to allow select aliens to remain in the United States either temporarily or permanently. During the previous two Administrations there has been a concerted effort to increase the number of removals by increasing the use of streamlined removal processes and decreasingly allowing voluntary departure and withdraws of application.

If Congress considers reforms to the immigration system, the criteria and mechanisms for removing aliens from, and authorizing aliens to remain in, the United States may become central issues.

Appendix A. Removals by Country: Top 10 Countries

Table A-1. Removals by Country
Top 10 Countries from FY2004 through FY2013

	2004	2005	2006	2007	2008	2009	2010	2011	2012	2013	Total
Total Removals	240,665	246,431	280,974	319,382	359,795	391,932	383,031	388,409	419,384	438,421	3,468,424
Mexico % of total	175,865 73.1%	169,03168.6%	186,726 66.5%	208,996 65.4%	247,263 68.7%	277,18570.7%	273,915 71.5%	289,347 74.5%	306,870 73.2%	314,904 71.8%	2,444,608 70.5%
Guatemala % of total	9,729 4.0%	14,5225.9%	20,527 7.3%	25,898 8.1%	27,527 7.7%	29,6417.6%	29,710 7.8%	30,343 7.8%	38,677 9.2%	46,866 10.7%	273,662 7.9%
Honduras % of total	8,752 3.6%	15,5726.3%	27,060 9.6%	29,737 9.3%	28,885 8.0%	27,2837.0%	25,121 6.6%	22,028 5.7%	31,515 7.5%	36,526 8.3%	252,703 7.3%
El Salvador % of total	7,269 3.0%	8,305 3.4%	11,050 3.9%	20,045 6.3%	20,050 5.6%	20,8445.3%	20,347 5.3%	17,381 4.5%	18,677 4.5%	20,862 4.8%	165,146 4.8%
Brazil % of total	6,390 2.7%	7,0972.9%	4,217 1.5%	4,210 1.3%	3,836 1.1%	3,7241.0%	3,533 0.9%	3,350 0.9%	2,256 0.5%	1,411 0.3%	40,165 1.2%
Dominican Republic % of total	3,760 1.6%	3,2101.3%	3,107 1.1%	2,990 0.9%	3,232 0.9%	3,5760.9%	3,371 0.9%	2,893 0.7%	2,833 0.7%	2,278 0.5%	31,285 0.9%
Colombia % of total	2,725 1.1%	2,5941.1%	2,788 1.0%	2,993 0.9%	2,590 0.7%	2,7140.7%	2,403 0.6%	1,900 0.5%	1,499 0.4%	1,421 0.3%	23,718 0.7%
Ecuador % of total	1,116 0.5%	1,4900.6%	1,750 0.6%	1,564 0.5%	2,330 0.6%	2,3830.6%	2,385 0.6%	1,716 0.4%	1,720 0.4%	1,491 0.3%	17,988 0.5%
Nicaragua %	947	1,2920.5%	2,446	2,307	2,257	2,1720.6%	1,903	1,502	1,373	1,337	17,563

	2004	2005	2006	2007	2008	2009	2010	2011	2012	2013	Total
of total	0.4%		0.9%	0.7%	0.6%		0.5%	0.4%	0.3%	0.3%	0.5%
Jamaica % of total	2,541 1.1%	2,0230.8%	1,662 0.6%	1,490 0.5%	1,628 0.5%	1,6620.4%	1,483 0.4%	1,475 0.4%	1,311 0.3%	1,101 0.3%	16,383 0.5%

Source: CRS analysis of Department of Homeland Security, Office of Immigration Statistics, Yearbook of Immigration Statistics: 2013, Washington, DC, Table 41.

APPENDIX B. TYPES OF CANCELLATION OF REMOVAL

Cancellation of removal was created in the Illegal Immigration Reform and Immigrant Responsibility Act of 1996 (IIRIRA, P.L. 104-208). It replaced two other forms of relief from removal,[134] and the eligibility requirements are generally tighter for those who do not have LPR status than they were in the forms of relief it replaced.[135] Certain aliens are ineligible for cancellation of removal, including those who are removable on security or terrorism grounds and those who have previously received cancellation of removal.[136]

INA §240A(a) gives the Attorney General the ability to cancel the removal of an alien who is inadmissible or deportable and adjust the alien's status to LPR if the alien

- has been an LPR for at least five years,
- has resided in the United States continuously[137] for seven years after being admitted[138] as an LPR, and
- has not been convicted of an aggravated felony.[139]

The Attorney General may also cancel the removal of an alien who is inadmissible or deportable and adjust the alien's status to LPR if the alien

- has been physically present in the United States for a continuous period of 10 years prior to the date of application for relief;
- has been a person of good moral character;[140]
- has not been convicted of a criminal offense that would make the alien inadmissible or deportable, or convicted of an offense related to document fraud or falsely claiming citizenship; and
- establishes that removal would result in *exceptional and extremely unusual hardship* to the alien's spouse, parent, or child who is a U.S. citizen or LPR (i.e., the hardship cannot be to the alien).

There are special rules for battered alien spouses and children.[141] Specifically, the Attorney General may cancel the removal of a battered alien spouse or child who is inadmissible or deportable and adjust the alien's status to LPR if the alien

- has been physically present in the United States for a continuous period of at least three years immediately preceding the date of such application;[142]
- has been a person of good moral character;[143]
- is not inadmissible on criminal or security grounds, or deportable for marriage fraud, criminal offenses, false documents, or security grounds; and has not been convicted of an aggravated felony; and
- establishes that the removal would result in *extreme hardship* to the alien, the alien's child, or the alien's parent.

Extreme hardship is evaluated on an individual basis, taking into account the particular facts and circumstances of each case. To establish extreme hardship, an applicant must demonstrate that deportation would result in a degree of hardship beyond that typically associated with deportation. Under regulation, applicants are encouraged to cite and document all applicable factors in their applications for cancellation of removal, as the presence or absence of any one factor may not be determinative in evaluating extreme hardship. Adjudicators should weigh all relevant factors presented and consider them in light of the totality of the circumstances.[144]

The Nicaraguan Adjustment and Central American Relief Act (NACARA) created a special cancelation of removal provision for certain Central Americans and Eastern Europeans.[145] This provision generally mirrors the suspension of deportation relief that was available before the enactment of IIRIRA in 1996. Reportedly, USCIS believes that nearly all qualifying NACARA applications have been adjudicated.[146]

End Notes

[1] An alien is anyone who is not a citizen or national of the United States. It is synonymous with noncitizen and foreign national. Unauthorized aliens are aliens who enter the country without inspection, aliens who enter with fraudulent documents, and aliens who enter legally but overstay the terms of their temporary visas.

[2] Bryan Baker and Nancy Rytina, Estimates of the Unauthorized Immigrant Population Residing in the United States: January 2012, Department of Homeland Security, Office of Immigration Statistics, March 2013.

[3] A lawful permanent resident (LPR) is a foreign national who is admitted into the United States to live lawfully and permanently in the country. LPR is synonymous with immigrant.

[4] A formal removal is one where the alien undergoes one of the removal procedures outlined in statute (e.g., expedited removal, removal hearings before an immigration judge). Generally, foreign nationals who undergo a formal removal process are barred from reentering the

United States for a certain amount of time. Other removable aliens may depart from the United States under the statutory authority of Voluntary Departure (return) or be allowed to withdraw their applications for admittance. These are often referred to as "returns" rather than removals.

[5] 8 U.S.C. 1101 et seq.

[6] Between 1940 and 2003, the primary authority to interpret, implement, and enforce the INA was vested with the Attorney General. With the implementation of the Homeland Security Act (P.L. 107-296) in 2003, the DHS Secretary became responsible for the administration and enforcement of most provisions of the INA, but the Attorney General retained responsibility for the adjudication of immigration removal cases through the Executive Office for Immigration Review (EOIR). Thus, removal is an area where the Attorney General and Secretary of Homeland Security both appear to have significant authority. For example, the Secretary of Homeland Security, generally through Immigration and Customs Enforcement (ICE) and Customs and Border Patrol (CBP), has authority over several types of expedited removal procedures, and decides which aliens the government will attempt to remove. The Attorney General, through EOIR, has ultimate authority over the immigration courts that preside over removal cases.

[7] INA §§235, 238, 240.

[8] In addition to renaming the grounds for excludability as grounds for inadmissibility, IIRIRA also reclassified unauthorized aliens who enter the United States without inspection as inadmissible (i.e., rather than deportable, as had been the case prior to IIRIRA).

[9] Inadmissible aliens have not been admitted to the United States and are ineligible to be admitted legally. An alien may be present in the United States but not admitted. For example, if an alien entered the United States without being inspected by an immigration officer, the alien would be physically present in the United States, but would not have been admitted. (Such an alien would be considered illegally present.) The INA also creates a distinction between "arriving aliens" and others, but does not define the term. Under regulations, an arriving alien is one who seeks admission or to transit through the United States, or who is interdicted and brought to the United States (8 C.F.R. 1.1(q)). Arriving aliens are ineligible for certain types of relief from removal.

[10] Deportable aliens have been inspected and admitted to the United States, but subsequently have become ineligible to remain and are subject to removal.

[11] Washington State Supreme Court, Gender and Justice Commission and Minority and Justice Commission, Immigration Resource Guide for Judges, July 2013.

[12] For more information on waivers for the grounds of inadmissibility, see CRS Report R41104, Immigration Visa Issuances and Grounds for Exclusion: Policy and Trends, by Ruth Ellen Wasem.

[13] Since its enactment in 1952, the INA has given the Attorney General and more recently the Secretary of Homeland Security prosecutorial discretion to exercise the power to remove foreign nationals. For more on the history of prosecutorial discretion, see U.S. Congress, House Committee on Homeland Security, Subcommittee on Border and Maritime Security, Does Administrative Amnesty Harm our Efforts to Gain and Maintain Operational Control of the Border?, Testimony of Ruth Ellen Wasem, Specialist in Immigration, Congressional Research Service, 112th Cong., 1st sess., October 4, 2011.

[14] See "Relief from Removal" in this report.

[15] Grounds of removal mean both the grounds of inadmissibility and deportability.

[16] For further discussion of the grounds of inadmissibility, see CRS Report R41104, Immigration Visa Issuances and Grounds for Exclusion: Policy and Trends, by Ruth Ellen Wasem.

[17] INA §212(a)(1). The INA does not define "communicable disease of public health significance," tasking the Secretary of Health and Human Services (HHS) to do so by regulation. For further discussion, see CRS Report R40570, Immigration Policies and Issues on Health-Related Grounds for Exclusion, by Ruth Ellen Wasem.

[18] INA §212(a)(2). For further discussion, see CRS Report RL32480, Immigration Consequences of Criminal Activity, by Michael John Garcia.

[19] INA §212(a)(3). For further discussion, see CRS Report RL32564, Immigration: Terrorist Grounds for Exclusion and Removal of Aliens, by Michael John Garcia and Ruth Ellen Wasem.

[20] INA §212(a)(4).

[21] INA §212(a)(5). For further discussion, see CRS Report RL33977, Immigration of Foreign Workers: Labor Market Tests and Protections, by Ruth Ellen Wasem.

[22] INA §212(a)(6)-(7).

[23] INA S212(a)(8). Although the ground "ineligible for citizenship" suggests a range of criteria linked to the naturalization provisions in Title III of the INA, its actual effect is to bar the entry of individuals who deserted their military service or evaded the military draft. For further discussion, see CRS Report R41104, Immigration Visa Issuances and Grounds for Exclusion: Policy and Trends, by Ruth Ellen Wasem, p. 16. See also CRS Report R42924, Prosecutorial Discretion in Immigration Enforcement: Legal Issues, by Kate M. Manuel and Todd Garvey.

[24] INA §212(a)(9). The reason for and type of removal determine the period of inadmissibility; see, "Consequences of an Order of Removal" in this report.

[25] INA §240(c)(3)(A).

[26] INA §237(a)(1). In other words, any alien who was admitted, but was inadmissible at the time of entry, is removable. Violations of immigration status include remaining in the United States past the authorized period of admission (i.e., overstaying a visa), and working in the United States under a visa category that does not permit employment.

[27] INA §237(a)(2). For further discussion, see CRS Report RL32480, Immigration Consequences of Criminal Activity, by Michael John Garcia.

[28] Moral turpitude is not defined under immigration law, and has been determined by case law. In general, if a crime manifests an element of baseness, vileness, or depravity under current mores—if it evidences an evil or predatory intent—it involves moral turpitude. For example, crimes such as murder, rape, blackmail, tax evasion, and fraud have been considered to involve moral turpitude, whereas crimes such as simple assault, possessing stolen property, and forgery have not. The flexibility in the term is to allow for changing social norms. For further discussion, see ibid. For a list of crimes that are considered to involve moral turpitude for the purpose of having a visa issued, see Department of State, Foreign Affairs Manual, vol. 9, §40.21(a).

[29] The definition of aggravated felony, in INA §101(a)(43), includes over 50 types of crimes. An alien convicted of an aggravated felony is conclusively presumed to be deportable (INA §238(c)). Misdemeanors at the state level may be aggravated felonies under the INA. For further discussion, see CRS Report RL32480, Immigration Consequences of Criminal Activity, by Michael John Garcia.

[30] INA §237(a)(3).

[31] INA §237(a)(4).

[32] INA §237(a)(5).

[33] INA §237(a)(6).

[34] Pursuant to INA §241(a)(2), aliens order removed on the basis of criminal offenses, terrorism, or security concerns always must be detained until the removal order is executed.

[35] Most of these requirements are prescribed in regulations, but under law the alien must be required to: (1) appear periodically before an immigration officer; (2) submit, if necessary, to a medical and psychiatric examination; (3) provide information under oath that the Secretary of DHS deems appropriate; and (4) obey reasonable written restrictions on conduct and activities as prescribed by the Secretary. (INA §241(a)(3); 8 C.F.R. §241.5) In addition, INA §241(a)(6) permits the continued detention past the removal period of inadmissible aliens, aliens ordered removed under criminal or terrorist grounds, or aliens who are determined to be a risk to the community or unlikely to comply with the removal order.

[36] INA §212(a)(9)(C).

[37] INA §212(a)(9). Pursuant to INA§212(a)(9)(B), an alien who is not ordered removed and who departs the country after being unlawfully present for at least six months is inadmissible for three years; and an alien unlawfully present for at least one year is inadmissible for 10 years. Both of these grounds for inadmissibility may be waived under certain circumstances. For further discussion, see CRS Report R41104, Immigration Visa Issuances and Grounds for Exclusion: Policy and Trends, by Ruth Ellen Wasem.

[38] Unlawful presence is only a criminal offense when an alien is found in the United States after having been formally removed or after departing the United States while a removal order was outstanding; see CRS Report RL32480, Immigration Consequences of Criminal Activity, by Michael John Garcia. The INA also includes certain criminal violations that may be prosecuted in federal district courts. These violations, which are beyond the scope of this report, include the bringing in and harboring of certain undocumented aliens (INA §274), the illegal entry of aliens (INA §275), and the reentry of aliens previously excluded or deported (INA §276), among others.

[39] INA §237(a)(1)(B).

[40] INA §240(b)(4)(A).

[41] For example, an action that does not make an alien removable at the time it occurs may make the alien deportable at a later date if Congress changes the law. See Charles Gordon, Stanley Mailman, Stephen Yale-Loehr, Immigration Law and Procedure. Newark: LexisNexis, vol. 6.

[42] DHS personnel authorized to issue a NTA include U.S. Customs and Border Protection (CBP) officers and U.S. Border Patrol agents (within CBP), asylum and examination officers in U.S. Citizenship and Immigration Services (USCIS), and detention officers and other agents in U.S. Immigration and Customs Enforcement (ICE); see 8 C.F.R. §239.1(a).

[43] Under INA §236, any alien may be detained while awaiting a determination of removability. In addition, criminal aliens; national security risks; arriving aliens subject to expedited removal; and arriving aliens who appear inadmissible for other than document-related reasons must be detained while awaiting a determination of removability. For more information on detention, see CRS Report RL32369, Immigration-Related Detention, by Alison Siskin.

[44] In FY2012, of those released on bond or on their own recognizance, or who were never detained, 21% failed to appear for their removal hearings. U.S. Department of Justice, Executive Office for Immigration Review, FY2012 Statistical Year Book, Falls Church, VA, February 2013.

[45] Aliens removable as "alien terrorists" may also be removed through a special removal court proceeding (INA Title V) though no such court has ever convened as of the date of this report.

[46] INA §212(a)(6)(B), 8 U.S.C. §1182(a)(6)(B).

[47] INA §240(b)(7). Types of relief from removal include asylum, cancellation of removal, withhold of removal, adjustment to LPR status, or change to a nonimmigrant classification. (See "Relief from Removal.") Such an alien is also ineligible for most types of relief from removal for 10 years. (INA, §240(b)(7), 8 U.S.C. §1229a(b)(7)).

[48] If an alien in removal proceedings is eligible to adjust status immediately (i.e., the alien is eligible to adjust status because of a family or employment relationship and a visa number is available) the immigration judge has discretion to continue the removal proceeding until the visa petition is decided. According to policy, Immigration and Customs Enforcement is directed to transfer the A-files (the immigration files) of aliens in removal proceedings who have pending LPR petitions to U.S. Citizenship and Immigration Services (USCIS). USCIS tries to adjudicate an alien's petition within 45 days (or 30 days if the alien is detained). John Morton, Assistant Secretary, Guidance Regarding the Handling of Removal Proceedings of Aliens with Pending or Approved Applications or Petitions, Immigration and Customs Enforcement, Policy Memorandum, Washington, DC, August 20, 2010.

[49] In regards to removal, the BIA, located in Falls Church, Virginia, has nationwide jurisdiction to hear appeals from certain decisions rendered by immigration judges. The BIA decides most appeals by conducting a "paper review" of cases. BIA decisions are binding on immigration judges unless modified or overturned by the Attorney General or a federal court. Department of Justice, Board of Immigration Appeals, Washington, DC, November 2011, http://www.justice.gov/eoir/biainfo.htm.

[50] For a detailed discussion of judicial review of removal orders, see archived CRS Report 97-788, Immigration: Judicial Review of Removal Orders, by Larry M. Eig, archived and available from the author.

[51] See the Antiterrorism and Effective Death Penalty Act of 1996 (P.L. 104-132, §442) and Illegal Immigration Reform and Immigrant Responsibility Act of 1996 (P.L. 104-208, Division C, Title III, Subtitle A).

[52] For a detailed discussion of expedited removal, see archived CRS Report RL33109, Immigration Policy on Expedited Removal of Aliens, by Alison Siskin and Ruth Ellen Wasem.

[53] Under expedited removal, both administrative and judicial review are limited generally to cases in which the alien claims to be a U.S. citizen or to have been previously admitted as a legal permanent resident, refugee, or asylee.

[54] See CRS Report RL32621, U.S. Immigration Policy on Asylum Seekers, by Ruth Ellen Wasem.

[55] In addition, expedited removal does not apply to noncitizens entering with a passport from a Visa Waiver Program country (8 C.F.R. §§235.3(b)(5) 1235.3(b)(5)). For more on the Visa Waiver Program, see CRS Report RL32221, Visa Waiver Program, by Alison Siskin.

[56] Unaccompanied alien children are defined in statute as children who lack lawful immigration status in the United States, are under the age of 18, and are without a parent or legal guardian in the United States or for whom no parent or legal guardian in the United States is available to provide care and physical custody. 6 U.S.C. §279(g)(2). For more on the issue of unaccompanied alien children, see CRS Report R43599, Unaccompanied Alien Children: An Overview, by Lisa Seghetti, Alison Siskin, and Ruth Ellen Wasem; and CRS Report

R43623, Unaccompanied Alien Children—Legal Issues: Answers to Frequently Asked Questions, by Kate M. Manuel and Michael John Garcia.

[57] Paul Virtue, Unaccompanied Minors Subject to Expedited Removal, Immigration and Naturalization Service, Policy Memorandum, Washington, DC, August 21, 1997. Although the policy was implemented in 1997, it appears that it is still current.

[58] There are special expedited removal procedures for aliens who appear inadmissible on security and related grounds (INA §235(c), 8 U.S.C. §1225(c)).

[59] Although the INA references the Attorney General, due to the Homeland Security Act of 2002 (P.L. 107-296), expedited removal policy is being administered by the Secretary of Homeland Security.

[60] Parole is a term in the INA which means that the alien has been granted temporary permission to enter and be present in the United States. Parole does not constitute formal admission to the United States and parolees are required to leave when the parole expires, or if eligible, to be admitted in a lawful status.

[61] The INA states that "the term credible fear of persecution means that there is a significant possibility, taking into account the credibility of the statements made by the alien in support of the alien's claim and such other facts as are known to the officer, that the alien could establish eligibility for asylum ... " (INA §235(b)(1)(B)(v); 8 U.S.C. §1225). See CRS Report RL32621, U.S. Immigration Policy on Asylum Seekers, by Ruth Ellen Wasem.

[62] INA §212(a)(9)(A)(i), 8 U.S.C. §1182(a)(9)(A)(i).

[63] See CRS Report RL32480, Immigration Consequences of Criminal Activity, by Michael John Garcia.

[64] Under the INA aliens who are convicted of crimes must complete their criminal sentences before they can be removed from the United States. INA §241(a)(4)(A), 8 U.S.C. §1231(a)(4)(A).

[65] INA §236(c), 8 U.S.C. §1226(c). See CRS Report RL32369, Immigration-Related Detention, by Alison.

[66] INA §212(a)(9)(A)(ii), 8 U.S.C. §1182(a)(9)(A)(ii).

[67] This program was known as the Institutional Removal Program (IRP), and is now operated under ICE's Criminal Alien Program as the Institutional Hearing Program (IHP).

[68] INA §238(b), 8 U.S.C. §1228(b).

[69] Aggravated felonies for immigration purposes include any crime of violence for which the term of imprisonment is at least one year, any crime of theft or burglary for which the term of imprisonment is at least one year, and illegal trafficking in drugs, firearms, or destructive devices. The definition also provides a list of many specific crimes. See CRS Report RL32480, Immigration Consequences of Criminal Activity, by Michael John Garcia.

[70] INA §238(b)(4), 8 U.S.C. §1228(b)(4).

[71] INA §212(a)(9)(A)(i), 8 U.S.C. §1182(a)(9)(A)(i).

[72] INA §241(a)(5) states that an alien who has had a removal order reinstated, "is not eligible and may not apply for any relief under that Act." Under regulation such aliens are eligible for withholding of removal. 8 C.F.R. §§241.8(e), 1241.8(e). Withholding of Removal is relief that prevents removal to a country where the foreign national has a clear probability of suffering persecution based on race, religion, nationality, political opinion, or membership in a particular social group.

[73] INA §241(a)(5), 8 U.S.C. 1231(a)(5).

[74] Foreign nationals who are eligible to adjust status under the Nicaraguan Adjustment and Central American Relief Act (NACARA) or under the Haitian Refugee Immigration Fairness Act (HRIFA) are not subject to reinstatement. For more on NACARA and HRIFA,

see archived CRS Report 98-270, Immigration: Haitian Relief Issues and Legislation, and archived CRS Report 97-810, Central American Asylum Seekers: Impact of 1996 Immigration Law, by Ruth Ellen Wasem. The reports are available from the author.

75 The maximum time an alien who accepts voluntary departure could be allowed to remain in the United States is 120 days. 8 C.F.R. §240.25(c).

76 INA §240B, 8 U.S.C. 1229c.

77 8 C.F.R. §§240.25, 1240.26.

78 8 C.F.R. §240.25(c).

79 8 C.F.R. §1240.26(a).

80 Aliens under voluntary departure must admit that their entry was illegal and waive their right to an immigration hearing. Aliens under voluntary departure may apply for legal entry in the future.

81 8 C.F.R. §235.4 states, "nothing in this regulation shall be construed as to give an alien the right to withdraw his or her request for admission."

82 8 C.F.R. §235.4.

83 Aliens who withdraw their applications may be paroled into the country if circumstances warrant. 8 C.F.R. §235.4.

84 For a discussion of these trends, see CRS Report R42138, Border Security: Immigration Enforcement Between Ports of Entry, by Lisa Seghetti.

85 P.L. 104-208, Title IV.

86 Muzaffar Chishti and Claire Bergeron, Post-9/11 Policies Dramatically Alter the U.S. Immigration Landscape, Migration Policy Institute, Policy Beat, Washington, DC, September 8, 2011, http://www.migrationpolicy.org/article/ post-911-policies-dramatically-alter-us-immigration-landscape.

87 Between FY2004 and FY2014, appropriations for CBP increased from $4.9 billion to $12.2 billion, and funding for ICE increased from $3.4 billion to $5.6 billion. CRS analysis of P.L. 113-76 and P.L. 108-90.

88 Department of Homeland Security, "DHS Released End of Year Statistics," press release, December 19, 2014; and Department of Homeland Security, Office of Immigration Statistics, Yearbook of Immigration Statistics: 2013, Washington, DC, Table 39; http://www.dhs.gov/yearbook-immigration-statistics-2013-enforcement-actions.

89 For more information on apprehensions and the Border Patrol, see CRS Report R42138, Border Security: Immigration Enforcement Between Ports of Entry, by Lisa Seghetti.

90 Non-Mexican nationals accounted for 36% of apprehensions in FY2013, 27% of apprehensions in FY2012, and 16% of apprehensions in FY2011. For FY2014 data: CRS analysis of data from U.S. Customs and Border Protection, CBP Border Security Report: Fiscal Year 2014, Washington, DC, December 19, 2014, p. 1. For FY2013 data see Customs and Border Protection, United States Border Patrol, Sector Profile- Fiscal Year 2013, http://www.cbp.gov/sites/
default/files/documents/U.S.%20Border%20Patrol%20Fiscal%20Year%202013%20Profile.pdf. For FY2011and FY2012 data see John F. Simanski and Lesley M. Sapp, Immigration Enforcement Actions: 2012, Department of Homeland Security, Office of Immigration Statistics, Washington, DC, December 2013, p. 3. For FY2010 CRS performed an analysis of unpublished data from CBP.

91 For a discussion of the Consequence Delivery System, see CRS Report R42138, Border Security: Immigration Enforcement Between Ports of Entry, by Lisa Seghetti.

[92] For a discussion of the expansion of expedited removal, see CRS Report RL33109, Immigration Policy on Expedited Removal of Aliens, by Alison Siskin and Ruth Ellen Wasem.

[93] CRS analysis of unpublished data provided by ICE.

[94] Between FY2012 and FY2013, the number of removals decreased from 346,487 to 332,538 (4%), while the number of returns decreased from 63,362 to 36,106 (43%). CRS analysis of unpublished data from DHS ICE.

[95] EOIR considers voluntary departure a removal in their statistics. U.S. Department of Justice, Executive Office for Immigration Review, FY2013 Statistical Year Book, Falls Church, VA, April 2014, p. 01.

[96] U.S. Department of Justice, Executive Office for Immigration Review, FY2013 Statistical Year Book, Falls Church, VA, April 2014, pp. C2-C5.

[97] An administrative closure is the temporary removal of a case from an immigration judge's calendar.

[98] 8 C.F.R. §204.21(c)(2).

[99] Total number of completions (i.e., when the immigration judge makes a determination) was 173,018 and 68,566 contained applications for relief from removal. U.S. Department of Justice, Executive Office for Immigration Review, FY2013 Statistical Year Book, Falls Church, VA, April 2014, p. I1.

[100] For a discussion of cancellation of removal in the context of possible legalization, see CRS Report R42958, Unauthorized Aliens: Policy Options for Providing Targeted Immigration Relief, by Andorra Bruno.

[101] In statute this is called cancellation of removal for nonpermanent residents.

[102] There are also special rules for cancellation of removal for Nicaraguan Adjustment and Central American Relief Act (NACARA) beneficiaries and battered alien spouses and children. See archived CRS Report 98-3, The Nicaraguan Adjustment and Central American Relief Act: Hardship Relief and Long-Term Illegal Aliens, by Larry M. Eig, and CRS Report R42477, Immigration Provisions of the Violence Against Women Act (VAWA), by William A. Kandel.

[103] Factors that may be considered favorable to an alien's request for cancellation of removal include the alien's family ties in the United States, service in the U.S. Armed Forces, history of employment, evidence of business ties, and proof of rehabilitation if a criminal record exists. Gordon, Charles, et al., Immigration Law and Procedure §64.04[2][b][iii].

[104] If the cap is reached, the immigration judge or BIA can reserve decisions until the next fiscal year for cases that merit relief.

[105] The number of cancellation of removal grants for non-LPRs includes 282 cases that were not subject to the numerical limits, and 15 cases that were technically suspensions of deportation. U.S. Department of Justice, Executive Office for Immigration Review, FY2013 Statistical Year Book, Falls Church, VA, April 2014, p. N1.

[106] This section is adapted from CRS Report R41753, Asylum and "Credible Fear" Issues in U.S. Immigration Policy, by Ruth Ellen Wasem.

[107] INA §208; 8 U.S.C. §1158.

[108] INA §208(b)(2); 8 U.S.C. §1158.

[109] The grant rate is calculated using the number of defensive asylum applications that were either denied or granted during FY2013. Notably, the number of grants and denials differs from the number of applications for several reasons. First, some cases are adjudicated in a different year from when the application is received; and secondly, not all cases end with a ruling by an immigration judge (e.g., withdraws, administrative closures.) U.S. Department

of Justice, Executive Office of Immigration Review, FY 2013 Statistical Yearbook, Falls Church, VA, April, 2014, pp. I1, K3.

[110] For a fuller discussion of adjustment of status, see CRS Report R42958, Unauthorized Aliens: Policy Options for Providing Targeted Immigration Relief, by Andorra Bruno.

[111] U.S. Department of Justice, Executive Office of Immigration Review, FY 2013 Statistical Yearbook, Falls Church, VA, April, 2014, p. N1.

[112] For more on the differences between asylum and withholding of removal, see CRS Report RL32480, Immigration Consequences of Criminal Activity, by Michael John Garcia.

[113] INA §214(b)(3), 8 U.S.C. §1231(b)(3).

[114] This form of relief fulfills the United States' obligations as a party to the 1967 United Nations Protocol Relating to the Status of Refugees.

[115] For a discussion on this provision, see U.S. Department of Justice, Executive Office of Immigration Review, FY 2013 Statistical Yearbook, Falls Church, VA, April 2014, p K5.

[116] The INA states that an alien who has been convicted of an aggravated felony (or felonies) for which the alien has been sentenced to an aggregate term of imprisonment of at least five years is considered to have committed a particularly serious crime. INA §214(b)(3)(B), 8 U.S.C. §1231(b)(3)(B).

[117] Unlike asylum, not all aggravated felonies automatically make an alien ineligible for withholding of removal. To be ineligible for withholding of removal, the alien must have been convicted of one or more aggravated felonies for which the aggregate sentence imposed was five years or more. INA §241(b)(3); 8 U.S.C. §1231(b)(3).

[118] U.S. Department of Justice, Executive Office for Immigration Review, FY2013 Statistical Year Book, Falls Church, VA, April 2014, p. K5.

[119] Grants of asylum and withholding of removal tend to be jointly considered. In FY2013, there was a grant rate of 61% for asylum and withholding of removal. U.S. Department of Justice, Executive Office for Immigration Review, FY2012 Statistical Year Book, Falls Church, VA, April 2014, p. K6.

[120] For more information on CAT see, CRS Report RL32276, The U.N. Convention Against Torture: Overview of U.S. Implementation Policy Concerning the Removal of Aliens, by Michael John Garcia.

[121] Regulations define torture as "any act by which severe pain or suffering, whether physical or mental, is intentionally inflicted on a person for such purposes as obtaining from him or her or a third person information or a confession, punishing him or her for an act he or she or a third person has committed or is suspected of having committed, or intimidating or coercing him or her or a third person, or for any reason based on discrimination of any kind, when such pain or suffering is inflicted by or at the instigation of or with the consent or acquiescence of a public official or other person acting in an official capacity." 8 C.F.R. §1208.18(a)(1). For a full legal analysis of the Torture Convention, see CRS Report RL32276, The U.N. Convention Against Torture: Overview of U.S. Implementation Policy Concerning the Removal of Aliens, by Michael John Garcia.

[122] Technically, relief under CAT is granted through the withholding of removal or deferral of removal. Unless the alien is of a class subject to mandatory denial of withholding of removal on security, criminal, or related grounds, CAT-based relief is granted in the form of withholding of removal. Aliens who are not eligible for withholding of removal are granted deferral of removal. 8 C.F.R. §1208.16(c)(4) and §1208.17.

[123] U.S. Department of Justice, Executive Office for Immigration Review, FY2013 Statistical Year Book, Falls Church, VA, April 2014, p. M1.

[124] This section is adapted from CRS Report RS20844, Temporary Protected Status: Current Immigration Policy and Issues, by Lisa Seghetti, Karma Ester, and Ruth Ellen Wasem.

[125] INA §244(h); 8 U.S.C. §1254a.

[126] 8 U.S.C. §240.

[127] INA §244(h); 8 U.S.C. §1254a.

[128] The countries are El Salvador, Guinea, Haiti, Honduras, Liberia, Nicaragua, Sierra Leone, Somalia, Sudan, South Sudan, and Syria. U.S. Citizenship and Immigration Services, Temporary Protected Status, Washington, DC, January 7, 2015; http://www.uscis.gov/humanitarian/temporary-protected-status-deferred-enforced-departure/temporaryprotected-status#Countries Currently Designated for TPS.

[129] For example, see United States Citizenship and Immigration Services, "Deferred Enforced Departure," October 13, 2011.

[130] Liberians were originally given DED by President George W. Bush on October 1, 2007. Most recently, on September 26, 2014, President Barack Obama extended DED for Liberians until September 30, 2016. The White House, Office of the Press Secretary, "Presidential Memorandum—Deferred Enforced Departure for Liberians," press release, September 26, 2014.

[131] Deferred action was originally known as "nonpriority." For a fuller discussion of deferred action, see Andorra Bruno, Todd Garvey, and Kate Manuel, et al., Analysis of June 15, 2012 DHS Memorandum, Exercising Prosecutorial Discretion with Respect to Individuals Who Came to the United States as Children, Congressional Research Service, Congressional Distribution Memorandum, July 13, 2012.

[132] Charles Gordon, Stanley Mailman, and Stephen Yale-Loehr, et al., Immigration Law and Procedure, vol. 6, Section 72.03[2][h].

[133] For a discussion of DACA, see CRS Report R43747, Deferred Action for Childhood Arrivals (DACA): Frequently Asked Questions, by Andorra Bruno.

[134] Relief under former INA §212(c) and suspension of deportation.

[135] For a discussion of the changes made by the 1996 Act, see CRS Report 97-911, Suspension of Deportation: Tighter Standards and Their Application to Central Americans and Other Long-Term Residents, by Larry M. Eig, and CRS Report 97-810, Central American Asylum Seekers: Impact of 1996 Immigration Law, by Ruth Ellen Wasem. Both reports are archived and available from the authors.

[136] Other aliens who are ineligible for cancellation of removal include aliens who entered as crewmen before June 30, 1964; aliens who were admitted as cultural exchange visitors (J visa holders) and did not fulfill their two-year home residency requirement; aliens admitted as exchange visitors to receive graduate medical education or training; or aliens who ordered, incited, assisted or otherwise participated in the persecution of others based on their race, religion, nationality, membership in a social group, or political opinion. (INA §240a(c); 8 U.S.C. §1229b(c)).

[137] Continuous residence ends when the alien is served an NTA or commits an offense that makes him or her removable. In addition, aliens who have served at least 24 months of active duty in the armed forces are exempted from the continuous residence requirement. (INA §240A(d); 8 U.S.C. §1229b(d)).

[138] Admission is defined in INA §101(a)(13) as "lawful entry into the United States after inspection and authorization by an immigration officer."

[139] Although the INA does not require a specific showing of hardship, the factors that guide the judge's exercise of discretion are similar to the factors required to demonstrate hardship. Gordon, Charles, et al., Immigration Law and Procedure §64.04[2][b].

[140] INA §101(f) lists characteristics that would preclude one from being found to have good moral character, but it does not provide an all-encompassing definition of the acts that could cause a person to be found to lack a "good moral character." Included in the preclusions found in INA §101(f) are being a habitual drunkard, having income derived primarily from gambling, giving false testimony to gain an immigration benefit, or having been convicted and confined to prison for an aggregate of 180 days.

[141] To qualify for cancellation of removal as a battered spouse or child, the alien must establish that he/she:

- has been battered or subjected to extreme cruelty by a spouse or parent who is or was a United States citizen (or is the parent of a child of a United States citizen and the child has been battered or subjected to extreme cruelty by such citizen parent);
- has been battered or subjected to extreme cruelty by a spouse or parent who is or was a lawful permanent resident (or is the parent of a child of an alien who is or was a lawful permanent resident and the child has been battered or subjected to extreme cruelty by such permanent resident parent); or
- has been battered or subjected to extreme cruelty by a United States citizen or lawful permanent resident whom the alien intended to marry, but whose marriage is not legitimate because of that United States citizen's or lawful permanent resident's bigamy. (INA §240A(b)(2)(A)(i); 8 U.S.C. §1229b(b)(2)(A)(i))

  The special provisions related to battered aliens were enacted as part of the Violence Against Women Act of 1994 (VAWA; P.L. 103-322) and the Violence Against Women Act of 2000 (P.L. 106-386). For more on the immigration provisions in VAWA, see CRS Report R42477, Immigration Provisions of the Violence Against Women Act (VAWA), by William A. Kandel.

[142] The alien is not considered to have failed to maintain continuous physical presence by reason of an absence if the alien can demonstrate a connection between the absence and the battery or extreme cruelty. (INA §240A(b)(2)(B); 8 U.S.C. §1229b(b)(2)(B)).

[143] The Attorney General may waive the good moral character requirement if the act or conviction was connected to the alien's having been battered or subjected to extreme cruelty. (INA §240A(b)(2)(C); 8 U.S.C. §1229b(b)(2)(C)).

[144] 8 C.F.R. §1240.58.

[145] P.L. 105-100 as amended by P.L. 105-139, signed into law on December 2, 1997.

[146] Gordon, Charles, et al., Immigration Law and Procedure §64.04[7][a]. For more on the special cancellation of removal provisions for NACARA beneficiaries, see CRS Report 98-3, The Nicaraguan Adjustment and Central American Relief Act: Hardship Relief and Long-Term Illegal Aliens, by Larry M. Eig; and CRS Report 97-810, Central American Asylum Seekers Impact of 1996 Immigration Law, by Ruth Ellen Wasem (available from the author).

In: Removal and Exclusion of Foreign Nationals ISBN: 978-1-63482-610-5
Editor: Delia Gibson

Chapter 2

IMMIGRATION POLICIES AND ISSUES ON HEALTH-RELATED GROUNDS FOR EXCLUSION*

Ruth Ellen Wasem

SUMMARY

News of humans infected with Ebola in West Africa, avian influenza in China, polio in the Middle East, and dengue fever in the Caribbean are examples of reports that heighten concerns about the health screenings of people arriving in the United States. Under current law, foreign nationals who wish to come to the United States generally must obtain a visa and submit to an inspection to be admitted. One of the reasons why a foreign national might be deemed inadmissible is on health-related grounds. The diseases that trigger inadmissibility in the Immigration and Nationality Act (INA) are those communicable diseases of public health significance as determined by the Secretary of Health and Human Services (HHS).

Currently there are seven diseases deemed a communicable disease of public health significance: chancroid, gonorrhea, granuloma inguinale, infectious leprosy, lymphogranuloma venereum, active tuberculosis, and infectious syphilis. Other diseases incorporated by reference are cholera; diphtheria; infectious tuberculosis; plague; smallpox; yellow fever; viral

* This is an edited, reformatted and augmented version of a Congressional Research Service publication R40570, prepared for Members and Committees of Congress dated August 13, 2014.

hemorrhagic fevers (Lassa, Marburg, Ebola, Crimean-Congo, South American, and others not yet isolated or named); severe acute respiratory syndrome (SARS); and "[i]nfluenza caused by novel or reemergent influenza viruses that are causing, or have the potential to cause, a pandemic." The INA also renders inadmissible foreign nationals who are not vaccinated against vaccine-preventable diseases. Vaccinations are statutorily required for mumps, measles, rubella, polio, tetanus, diphtheria, pertussis, influenza type B and hepatitis B. Vaccinations against other diseases may also be required if recommended by the Advisory Committee for Immunization Practices (ACIP).

The Centers for Disease Control and Prevention (CDC) in HHS take the lead in protection against communicable diseases among foreign nationals who come to the United States. The CDC are responsible for providing the technical instructions to civil surgeons and panel physicians who conduct medical examinations for immigration purposes. Foreign nationals who are applying for visas at U.S. consulates are tested by in-country physicians who have been designated by the State Department. The physicians enter into written agreements with the consular posts to perform the examinations according to HHS regulations and guidance. Foreign nationals in the United States who are adjusting to legal permanent resident status are tested by civil surgeons designated by U.S. Citizenship and Immigration Services, an agency within the Department of Homeland Security (DHS). CDC, in conjunction with Customs and Border Protection (CBP) in DHS, operates 20 quarantine stations and has health officials on call for all ports of entry.

From an immigration standpoint, an outbreak of an infectious disease places substantial procedural and resource pressures on CBP, which is charged with screening admissions of all travelers at land, sea, and air ports of entry (POE). CBP officers screened approximately 362 million individuals in FY2013 for admissions into the United States. CBP works in conjunction with the CDC to monitor travelers and attempt to contain any diseases that may be spread by travelers coming from abroad. In the current context of the Ebola outbreak in West Africa, CDC has emphasized exit-based airport screening from areas with Ebola, and not screening at POEs in the United States. At this point, CDC assures that Ebola poses little risk to the U.S. general population.

Congress has acted legislatively on the health-related grounds for exclusion several times in the recent past. Congress also plays an important oversight role, particularly when concerns arise regarding contagious diseases or potential pandemics.

INTRODUCTION

News of humans infected with Ebola in West Africa,[1] avian influenza in China, polio in the Middle East, and dengue fever in the Caribbean are examples of reports that heighten concerns about the health screenings of people arriving in the United States.[2] Worldwide migration has hit unprecedented levels, now roughly estimated at 214 million international migrants. The United States hosts millions of foreign nationals on a temporary basis and is the prospective home to 1 million lawful permanent residents each year.

Under current law, foreign nationals not already legally residing in the United States who wish to come to the United States generally must obtain a visa and submit to an inspection to be admitted.[3] They must first meet a set of criteria specified in the Immigration and Nationality Act (INA) that determine whether they are eligible for admission. Moreover, they must also not be deemed inadmissible according to specified grounds in the INA. One of the reasons why a foreign national might be deemed inadmissible is on health-related grounds.[4]

While grounds for exclusion based on health-related criteria have long existed in the Immigration and Nationality Act (INA), some have questioned whether these provisions are sufficient to deal with a potential pandemic situation. Potential issues for Congress are at least three-fold: (1) Are the health-related grounds for exclusion updated to ensure public safety in regards to contagious diseases? (2) Would increasing restrictions on foreign travel (even temporarily) during potential pandemics inflict more of an economic harm than a benefit? (3) Are the resources provided for frontline agencies charged with screening foreign travelers adequate to identify potentially infected travelers?

The Department of State (DOS) and the Department of Homeland Security (DHS) each play key roles in administering the law and policies on the admission of aliens.[5] DOS's Bureau of Consular Affairs (Consular Affairs) is the agency responsible for issuing visas, DHS's U.S. Citizenship and Immigration Services (USCIS) is charged with approving immigrant petitions, and DHS's Customs and Border Protection (CBP) is tasked with inspecting all people who enter the United States. The Secretary of Health and Human Services (HHS) determines those communicable diseases of public health significance that trigger inadmissibility in the INA. The Centers for Disease Control and Prevention (CDC) in HHS take the lead in protection against communicable diseases among foreign nationals who come to the United States.

HEALTH-RELATED GROUNDS FOR EXCLUSION

With certain exceptions,[6] aliens seeking admission to the United States must undergo separate reviews performed by DOS consular officers abroad as well as CBP inspectors upon entry to the United States.[7] These reviews are intended to ensure that applicants are not ineligible for visas or admission under the grounds for inadmissibility spelled out in the INA.[8] These criteria are: health-related grounds; criminal history;[9] security and terrorist concerns; public charge (e.g., indigence); seeking to work without proper labor certification; illegal entry and immigration law violations; ineligible for citizenship; and aliens previously removed. The health-related grounds are further broken down into four categories: having a communicable disease, lacking required vaccinations, presenting a physical or mental disorder, and evidencing drug abuse or addiction.[10]

LEGISLATIVE HISTORY

The statutory language permitting the exclusion of aliens on the basis of health or communicable diseases dates back to the Immigration Act of 1891. "Persons suffering from a loathsome or a dangerous contagious disease" were added to the grounds of exclusion, and the 1891 Act also required a medical inspection of all aliens arriving at ports of entry.[11] When the various immigration and citizenship laws were unified and codified as the Immigration and Nationality Act of 1952 (INA), the health-related grounds were seven of 31 grounds for exclusion.[12] One of these seven health-related grounds specified that aliens "afflicted with any dangerous contagious disease" would be excluded from the United States.

The Immigration Amendments Act of 1990 streamlined and modernized all of the grounds for inadmissibility into nine broad categories. At that time, Congress recodified the health-related ground for inadmissibility to include any alien "who is determined (in accordance with regulations prescribed by the Secretary of Health and Human Services) to have a communicable disease of public health significance."

In 1996, the Illegal Immigration Reform and Immigrant Responsibility Act of 1996 (IIRIRA) amended the INA to require prospective immigrants to demonstrate that they have been vaccinated against certain "vaccine-preventable" diseases. More specifically, §341 of the IIRIRA created a new basis of inadmissibility in §212(a) for failing to present evidence of vaccination against nine "vaccine-preventable diseases," namely mumps, measles, rubella, polio, tetanus, diphtheria, pertussis, influenza type B and hepatitis B.

HIV/AIDS

Much of the policy debate since 1990 centered on HIV/AIDS.[13] In 1993, Congress amended the health-related grounds for inadmissibility by adding the phrase: "which shall include infection with the etiologic agent for acquired immune deficiency syndrome."[14] In 2008, § 305 of P.L. 110- 293, the Tom Lantos and Henry J. Hyde United States Global Leadership Against HIV/AIDS, Tuberculosis, and Malaria Reauthorization Act of 2008, eliminated the language in the INA that statutorily barred foreign nationals with HIV/AIDS from entering the United States. This revision does not, however, entitle foreign nationals with HIV/AIDS to receive visas to enter the United States. On September 29, 2008, the DHS announced the publication of a final rule that grants consular officers the authority to grant nonimmigrant visas to otherwise eligible applicants who are HIV-positive and meet certain requirements. Visas issued under the final rule do not publicly identify any traveler as HIV-positive. The HIV-waiver final rule applies to foreigners who are HIV-positive and seek to enter the United States as visitors for up to 30 days. The CDC issued a final rule amending its regulations to remove HIV infection from the definition of "communicable disease of public health significance" and to remove references to HIV from the scope of medical examinations for aliens on November 2, 2009.

Specified Communicable Diseases

The INA renders inadmissible foreign nationals infected with a "communicable disease of public health significance."[15] While the INA does not define "communicable disease of public health significance" directly, it does task the Secretary of Health and Human Services (HHS) to define the term by regulation. The relevant regulation's definition expressly lists seven diseases as a "communicable disease of public health significance": chancroid, gonorrhea, granuloma inguinale, infectious leprosy, lymphogranuloma venereum, active tuberculosis,[16] and infectious syphilis.[17] However, this list is neither exclusive nor exhaustive because the regulatory definition also includes other diseases incorporated by reference to a Presidential Executive Order.[18] The relevant executive order lists cholera; diphtheria; infectious tuberculosis; plague; smallpox; yellow fever; viral hemorrhagic fevers (Lassa, Marburg, Ebola, Crimean-Congo, South American, and others not yet isolated or named); severe acute respiratory syndrome (SARS); and "[i]nfluenza caused by novel or reemergent influenza viruses that are causing, or have the potential to cause, a pandemic."[19]

Furthermore, the regulatory definition also includes communicable diseases that may pose a "public health emergency of international concern."[20] A disease rises to this level, and thus qualifies as a "communicable disease of public significance," if the CDC Director, after evaluating (1) the seriousness of the disease, (2) whether the emergence of the disease was unusual or unexpected, (3) the risk of the spread of the disease in the United States, and (4) the transmissibility and virulence of the disease,[21] determines that "a threat exists for [the disease's] importation into the United States" and the disease "may potentially affect the health of the American public."[22]

Tuberculosis (TB)

In recent years, tuberculosis (TB) has prompted greater concerns with health and screening officials in the United States, due in part to the development of drug resistant strains of the disease.[23] These developments have caused agencies such as the CDC to implement instructions and preparedness plans for screening and handling travelers to the United States infected with TB. About one-third of the world's population is infected with *Mycobacterium (M.) tuberculosis*, the bacterium that causes TB. The vast majority have so-called "latent TB" infections and are not contagious. A small percentage (approximately 9 million people) have "TB disease;" more than 1 million of them die from the disease each year. Many but not all persons with TB disease are contagious and can transmit the disease to others. Many persons with latent TB infections never experience TB disease, although latent infections can progress to disease at any time.[24]

The processing of Hmong refugees located in Thailand was temporarily halted in 2005 to ensure that the refugees had completed treatment for infectious tuberculosis before they came to the United States.[25] Additional concerns were raised in Spring 2007 when two individuals with drug-resistant TB disease were requested flagged by HHS for CBP interdiction. Despite this call for interdiction, both individuals were able to enter the United States through ports of entry. These incidents resulted in a reassessment of federal coordination and response regarding TB and other contagious diseases.[26]

Almost 10,000 cases of TB disease were reported in the United States in 2013. Almost 65% of these cases were among foreign-born persons; the case rate among foreign-born persons was approximately 13 times higher than among U.S.-born persons. Although the number of cases of TB disease has been on the decline among both U.S.-born and foreign-born persons, the proportion of cases among the foreign-born has risen steadily since 1993.[27]

As discussed below, medical screening for tuberculosis is required of all refugees and foreign nationals seeking LPR visas to live in the United States. However, CBP does not currently have any special provisions outside of its general procedures for TB screening at ports of entry. The majority of TB disease cases reported in the United States among foreign-born persons have been attributed to reactivation of latent TB infection acquired previously, with the rate reflecting TB incidence in their countries of origin.[28] Therefore, most of these persons would not have been ineligible for visas on health-related grounds, and would not have been symptomatic of the disease at the time of their arrival at a port of entry.

Medical Examinations for Visas

The Centers for Disease Control and Prevention (CDC) in HHS take the lead in protection against communicable diseases among foreign nationals who come to the United States. The CDC are responsible for providing technical instructions to civil surgeons and panel physicians who conduct medical examinations for immigration purposes. Foreign nationals who are applying for visas at U.S. consulates are tested by in-country physicians who have been designated by the State Department. The physicians enter into written agreements with the consular posts to perform the examinations according to HHS regulations and guidance. Foreign nationals in the United States who are adjusting to legal permanent resident (LPR) status are tested by civil surgeons designated by USCIS.

A medical examination is required of all foreign nationals seeking to come as legal permanent residents and refugees, and may be required of any alien seeking a nonimmigrant visa or admission at the port of entry. Foreign nationals are generally tested at their own expense, though the costs for refugees are covered by the U.S. government. If there is reason to suspect an infection, applicants for temporary admission as nonimmigrants (such as tourists, business travelers, temporary workers, and foreign students) are tested at the discretion of the consular officer or admitting CBP inspector. Children under 15 years of age are required to have a general physical examination and provide proof of immunizations, but they are not required to have the chest x-rays, blood tests, or HIV anti-body test.[29]

Policies and procedures established over the years by the CDC spell out the obligations of the physicians who are designated to conduct the medical examination to meet the statutory requirements of the INA. According to the CDC's technical guidance for the physicians performing the medical examination, they are required to make an assessment of the foreign national that includes a medical history, a review of other available records, a physical examination, and required diagnostic tests (more detailed information on these requirements are available in *Appendix B*).[30] Afterwards, CDC guidance says, the panel physician completes the DS-2053 form if the visa is being processed by consular officers abroad, or the civil surgeon completes I-693 form if the status adjustment is being processed by USCIS adjudicators within the United States. In general, the medical reports are valid for one year.

Mere presence of one of the designated diseases does not always lead to exclusion. After a visa applicant is found to be afflicted with TB disease, for example, the consular officer or USCIS adjudicator is to request the medical examiner to determine whether the tuberculosis is Class A (infectious), Class B-1 (clinically active, not infectious) Class B-2 (not clinically active) or Class B-3 (old or healed tuberculosis). A foreign national diagnosed with Class B-1 tuberculosis, is not automatically ineligible for LPR visa purposes; nor is a foreign national diagnosed with Class B1, B-2, or B-3 tuberculosis automatically ineligible for nonimmigrant (temporary) visa purposes.[31]

Waivers of the Health Grounds

The INA gives the Secretary of Homeland Security[32] the discretionary authority to waive some of the health-related grounds for inadmissibility under certain circumstances.[33] For example, foreign nationals infected with a communicable disease of public health significance can still be issued a waiver and admitted into the country if they are the spouse, unmarried son, unmarried daughter, minor unmarried lawfully adopted child, father, or mother of a U.S. citizen, alien lawfully admitted for permanent residence, or an alien issued an immigrant visa, or is a VAWA selfpetitioner.[34] Waivers are also available, under certain circumstances, for those inadmissible for lacking proper vaccination[35] and for those who have a physical or mental disorder.[36] The Secretary may also waive the application of any of the health-related grounds for inadmissibility if he finds it in "the national interest" to do so.[37]

The Department of State Visa Office reports that a total of 362 potential LPRs were initially denied a visa in FY2013 on the basis of a communicable disease of public health significance (e.g., cholera, infectious tuberculosis, HIV/AIDS). However, 377 people obtained waivers or overcame an initial denial based upon a communicable disease and were granted LPR visas in FY2013.[38] Comparable data from the Department of Homeland Security have not been made available.

When waivers are given to nonimmigrants, it is done on a case-by-case basis for up to 30 days, for such reasons as visiting a family member, short-term treatment, or attending conferences. The Department of State Visa Office reports that a total of 17 potential nonimmigrants were denied a visa in FY2013 on the basis of a communicable disease of public health significance. Also in FY2013, four people obtained waivers or overcame an initial denial based upon a communicable disease and received a nonimmigrant visa.[39] Comparable data from the Department of Homeland Security have not been made available.

Vaccination Requirements

As stated above, the INA renders inadmissible foreign nationals who are not vaccinated against vaccine-preventable diseases.[40] Vaccinations are statutorily required for mumps, measles, rubella, polio, tetanus, diphtheria, pertussis, influenza type B and hepatitis B. Vaccinations against other diseases may also be required if recommended by the Advisory Committee for Immunization Practices (ACIP), an advisory committee to the CDC.[41] Those vaccinations against other diseases the ACIP have added are hepatitis A, human papillomavirus, meningococcal, pneumococcal, rotavirus, varicella, zoster, and the annual influenza vaccine.[42] Most visas denied on this basis are overcome when evidence of the vaccination is presented.[43]

If the panel physician or civil surgeon believes that a vaccination record is fraudulent, the visa applicant is handled in the same way as someone who has failed to present a vaccination record. The vaccination requirement may be waived when the foreign nation receives the vaccination, the civil surgeon or panel physician certifies that the vaccination would not be medically appropriate, or if the vaccination would be contrary to the foreign national's religious or moral beliefs.[44]

PORT OF ENTRY PROCEDURES

There are 328 official ports of entry (POE) in the United States, including 16 preclearance offices in Canada, Ireland, the Caribbean, and the United Arab Emirates.[45] CBP officers screened approximately 362 million individuals in FY2013 for admissions into the United States. The vast majority of admissions into the United States occur at the land border, where local and regional economies are dependent upon the movement of goods and people across the border to maintain economic viability.[46] From the perspective of the CBP, the most significant challenge in screening for infectious diseases comes at the land border. Even without medical screening or other special circumstances, land borders can build up inspection lines that are several hours long due to the high demand for crossings and inadequate infrastructure at most POEs to accommodate such crossings.

As noted above, the CDC is the lead agency charged with protection against communicable diseases and is responsible for providing the technical instructions to civil surgeons and panel physicians who conduct medical examinations for immigration. CDC officials are not present at the border on a day-to-day basis, but there are quarantine stations located in a number of international airports and near a few land ports of entry (for a full list, see *Appendix A*). However, these 20 stations constitute a small fraction of the 329 ports of entry operated by CBP. Even fully staffed quarantine stations are not in a position to perform routine health screening on all passengers crossing the border as a standard operating procedure.

Rather than staffing all the POEs, the CDC, through their Division of Global Migration and Quarantine (DGMQ),[47] train CBP inspectors to watch for ill persons and items of public health concern. CDC approves the physicians used at the POEs, and the tests are performed in consultation with and in accordance with CDC guidance. CDC officials are to be stationed at the border during immigration emergencies and other periods when public health may be threatened.[48]

The CBP Inspector's Field Manual states that CBP officers are responsible for observing all travelers for obvious signs and symptoms of quarantinable and communicable diseases, such as (1) fever, which could be detected by a flushed complexion, shivering, or profuse sweating; (2) jaundice (unusual yellowing of skin and eyes); (3) respiratory problems, such as severe cough or difficulty breathing; (4) bleeding from the eyes, nose, gums, or ears or from wounds; and (5) unexplained weakness or paralysis.[49] Additionally, a person is considered to be ill in terms of foreign quarantine regulations when symptoms meet the following criteria:

1. Temperature of 100 degrees Fahrenheit or greater which is accompanied by one or more of the following: rash, jaundice, glandular swelling, or which has persisted for 2 days or more.
2. Diarrhea severe enough to interfere with normal activity or work.[50]

However, CBP officers are not medically trained or qualified to physically examine or diagnose illness among arriving travelers.

According to a Government Accountability Office (GAO) report,[51] there are three general scenarios in which CBP officers encounter ill persons who are in need of medical attention or who may pose a public health threat:

- In the most common scenario, CBP officers encounter an individual who discloses that he/she needs medical attention for various health reasons.
- CBP officers suspect an individual may need medical attention or may pose a public health risk to others (e.g., individual exhibits obvious signs and symptoms of illness, such as fever, weakness, or both, as observed by officers).
- CBP officers encounter an individual who is an exact match to a public health alert in Treasury Enforcement Communications System (TECS II)[52] and may pose a public health risk to others.

The GAO report additionally states that in all three scenarios, CBP protocols require officials, at a minimum, to isolate the person while notifying officials at CDC and, depending on the circumstance, to contact the designated local public health authorities.[53] Each port of entry, according to GAO, is supplied with personal protective equipment, including masks and gloves, and inspecting officers must use this equipment in dealing with travelers suspected of having communicable or quarantinable illnesses, as well as while handling the individuals' documents and belongings. CBP officers are responsible for coordinating with CDC to provide assistance in identifying arriving individuals from areas with known communicable disease outbreaks.

In the context of the current Ebola outbreak in West Africa, CDC has emphasized exit-based airport screening from areas of the source,[54] not POE screening in the United States. "When this has been evaluated, the yield is much, much greater to try to control the disease at the source, and control the screening and right close to the source. The vast majority of flights from this region to the United States are indirect."[55] At this point, CDC assures that Ebola poses little risk to the U.S. general population.[56]

APPENDIX A. CDC QUARANTINE STATIONS

Table A-1. CDC Quarantine Stations by City and Location

City	Location
Anchorage, AK	Ted Stevens Anchorage International Airport
Atlanta, GA	Hartsfield-Jackson Atlanta International Airport
Boston, MA	Logan International Airport
Chicago, IL	O'Hare International Airport
Dallas/Ft. Worth, TX	Dallas/Ft. Worth International Airport
Detroit, MI	Detroit Metro Airport
El Paso, TX	CDC El Paso Quarantine Station
Honolulu, HI	Honolulu International Airport
Houston, TX	George Bush Intercontinental Airport
Los Angeles, CA	Los Angeles International Airport
Miami, FL	Miami International Airport
Minneapolis, MN	Minneapolis-St. Paul International Airport
Newark, NJ	Newark Liberty International Airport
New York, NY	John F. Kennedy International Airport
Philadelphia, PA	Philadelphia International Airport
San Diego, CA	CDC San Diego Quarantine Station
San Francisco, CA	San Francisco International Airport

City	Location
San Juan, PR	Luis Muñoz Marin International Airport
Seattle, WA	Seattle-Tacoma International Airport
Washington, DC	Dulles International Airport

Source: CRS presentation of information posted on CDC website, available at http://www.cdc.gov/quarantine/ quarantine-stations-us.html.

Notes: Information is current as of April 14, 2014.

APPENDIX B. CDC TECHNICAL GUIDANCE

As previously discussed, policies and procedures established over the years by the CDC spell out the obligations of the physicians who are designated to conduct the medical examination to meet the statutory requirements of the INA. According to the CDC's technical guidance[57] for the physicians performing the medical examination, they are required to make the following assessments of the foreign nationals seeking visas:

- A medical history, obtained by the civil surgeon or a member of the physician's professional staff, from the applicant (preferably) or a family member, which includes (1) a review of all hospitalizations; (2) a review of all institutionalizations for chronic conditions (physical or mental); (3) a review of all illnesses or disabilities resulting in a substantial departure from a normal state of well-being or level of functioning; (4) specific questions about psychoactive drug and alcohol use, history of harmful behavior, and history of psychiatric illness not documented in the medical records reviewed; and (5) a review of chest radiographs and treatment records if the alien has a history suggestive of tuberculosis.
- A review of any other records that are available to the physician (e.g., police, military, school, or employment) that may help to determine a history of harmful behavior related to a physical or mental disorder and to determine whether illnesses or disabilities are present that result in a substantial departure from a normal state of well-being or level of functioning.
- A review of systems sufficient to assist in determining the presence and the severity of Class A or Class B conditions. The physician should ask specifically about symptoms that suggest cardiovascular,

pulmonary, musculoskeletal, and neuropsychiatric disorders. Symptoms suggestive of infection with any of the excludable communicable diseases (tuberculosis, HIV infection, syphilis, chancroid, gonorrhea, granuloma inguinale, lymphogranuloma venereum, and Hansen's disease) should also be sought.

- A physical examination, including an evaluation of mental status, sufficient to permit a determination of the presence and the severity of Class A and Class B conditions. The physical examination is to include a mental status examination that includes, at a minimum, assessment of intelligence, thought, cognition (comprehension), judgment, affect (and mood), and behavior.
- A physical examination that includes, at a minimum, examination of the eyes, ears, nose and throat, extremities, heart, lungs, abdomen, lymph nodes, skin and external genitalia.
- All diagnostic tests required for the diagnosis of the diseases identified as communicable diseases of public health significance and other tests identified as necessary to confirm a suspected diagnosis of any other Class A or Class B condition.

End Notes

[1] For more information, see CRS Report IF00044, Ebola: 2014 Outbreak in West Africa (In Focus), by Nicolas Cook and Tiaji Salaam-Blyther; and CRS Report IN10126, Safe at Home? Letting Ebola-Stricken Americans Return, by Sarah A. Lister.

[2] For the latest reports on epidemics and pandemics , see the Global Alert and Response (GAR) publications of the World Health Organization at http://www.who.int/ csr/resources /publications/en/ .

[3] Authorities to except or to waive visa requirements are specified in law, such as the broad parole authority of the Attorney General under §212(d)(5) of the Immigration and Nationality Act (INA) and the specific authority of the Visa Waiver Program in §217 of the INA.

[4] Other grounds for exclusion include criminal history; security and terrorist concerns; public charge (e.g., indigence); seeking to work without proper labor certification; illegal entry and immigration law violations; ineligible for citizenship; and aliens previously removed. For more information, see CRS Report RL32256, Visa Policy: Roles of the Departments of State and Homeland Security, by Ruth Ellen Wasem.

[5] Other departments, notably the Department of Labor (DOL), and the Department of Agriculture (USDA), play roles in the approval process depending on the category or type of visa sought, and the Department of Health and Human Services (HHS) sets policy on the health-related grounds for inadmissibility discussed below.

[6] Certain classes of aliens are not required to obtain a visa to enter the United States and are therefore exempt from the consular review process. For example, under the visa waiver

program (VWP), nationals from certain countries are permitted to enter the United States as temporary visitors (nonimmigrants) for business or pleasure without first obtaining a visa from a U.S. consulate abroad. See INA §217; 8 U.S.C. §1187. For additional background on the VWP, see CRS Report RL32221, Visa Waiver Program, by Alison Siskin.

[7] For background and analysis of alien screening and visa issuance policy, see CRS Report R41104, Immigration Visa Issuances and Grounds for Exclusion: Policy and Trends, by Ruth Ellen Wasem; and CRS Report R41093, Visa Security Policy: Roles of the Departments of State and Homeland Security, by Ruth Ellen Wasem.

[8] INA §212(a); 8 U.S.C. §1182(a).

[9] For a full discussion of this ground, see CRS Report RL32480, Immigration Consequences of Criminal Activity, by Michael John Garcia.

[10] INA §212(a)(1)(A).

[11] Act of March 3, 1891; 26 Stat. 1084.

[12] For a complete analysis of the pre-1990 laws and policies, see U.S. Congress, House Committee on the Judiciary, Grounds for Exclusion of Aliens under the Immigration and Nationality Act: Historical Background and Analysis, committee print, prepared by the Congressional Research Service, 100th Cong., 2nd sess., September 1988, Ser. No. 7.

[13] INA §212(a). The FY1987 Supplemental Appropriations Act included in §518 the following requirement: "On or before August 31, 1987, the President, pursuant to his existing power under section 212(a)(6) of the Immigration and Nationality Act, shall add human immunodeficiency virus infection to the list of dangerous contagious diseases contained in title 42 of the Code of Federal Regulations." Simultaneously with the vote, HHS published a final rule adding AIDS to the list of "dangerous contagious diseases" in Title 42 of the Code of Federal Regulations, and a proposed rule to replace AIDS on this list with HIV infection. Regulations implementing the statutory requirement were published by the HHS, effective August 31, 1987.

[14] P.L. 103-43, the National Institutes of Health Revitalization Act of 1993, §2007(a). The 1993 legislation was enacted in response to controversy over an announcement by the William Jefferson Clinton Administration that the HHS Public Health Service regulations would be revised to remove HIV infection and six other diseases from a list of diseases for which aliens could be excluded from the United States, leaving only infectious tuberculosis on the list. A similar amendment to the regulations had been proposed in January 1991, by the George H.W. Bush Administration, and had also been controversial. In both cases, the deletion of HIV infection from the list of excludable diseases caused the most concern. (June 10, 1993; 107 Stat. 210).

[15] INA §212(a)(1), 8 U.S.C. §1182(a)(1) (Any alien who is determined (in accordance with regulations prescribed by the Secretary of Health and Human Services) to have a communicable disease of public health significance ... is inadmissible.).

[16] The prevalence of active tuberculosis among foreign nationals has been a concern for many years. On January 23, 1991, HHS published a proposed rule in which infectious tuberculosis would have been the only communicable disease listed. That rule was suspended May 29, 1991, largely because of the controversies of leaving HIV/AIDS off the list.

[17] 42 C.F.R. §34.2(b).

[18] 42 C.F.R. §34.2(b)(2).

[19] Exec. Order. No. 13295, 68 FR 17255 (April 4, 2003) as amended by Exec. Order. No. 13375, 70 FR 17299 (April 1, 2005).

[20] 42 C.F.R. §34.2(b)(3).

[21] See 42 C.F.R. §34.3(d)(2) (factors used to determine whether a communicable disease poses a public health emergency of international concern).

[22] 42 C.F.R. §34.2(b)(3). See also Annex 2 of the revised International Health Regulations http://www.who.int/csr/ihr/ en.

[23] For more information on tuberculosis, see CRS Report RL34144, Extensively Drug-Resistant Tuberculosis (XDRTB): Emerging Public Health Threats and Quarantine and Isolation, by Kathleen S. Swendiman and Nancy Lee Jones.

[24] World Health Organization, "Tuberculosis Fact Sheet," March 2014, http:// www. who.int/mediacentre/factsheets/ fs104/en/; and Centers for Disease Control and Prevention, "The Difference Between Latent TB Infection and TB Disease," fact sheet, September 2012, http://www.cdc.gov/tb/publications/factsheets/general/LTBIandActiveTB.htm. U.S. Government Accountability Office, Public Health and Border Security: HHS and DHS Should Further Strengthen Their Ability to Respond to TB Incidents, GAO-09-58, October 2008, p. 1.

[25] "State Department Halts Travel of Hmong Refugees to U.S.; Institutes Enhanced Medical Screening," Interpreter Releases, vol. 82, no. 7 (February 14, 2005).

[26] According to a GAO report: "In the spring of 2007, HHS requested DHS's assistance in attempting to interdict at the border two individuals with drug-resistant TB disease so that they could direct them to treatment. According to HHS documents, in May 2007, one of these individuals, a U.S. citizen, traveled abroad against advice from physicians. When state and local health officials were unable to find this person and serve him with a written order not to travel, they requested help from HHS. While he was traveling abroad, HHS located him and attempted to direct him to treatment. HHS then contacted DHS for assistance. However, while HHS and DHS were determining a course of action to attempt to prevent him from traveling further by airplane, he once again traveled. Furthermore, as the departments were working to intercept him at the U.S. border, he was able to reenter the country because a U.S. Customs and Border Protection (CBP) officer, in violation of CBP policy, ignored a computerized alert in CBP's border screening and inspection system to detain him. In a separate incident, a Mexican citizen with drug-resistant TB who had a prior history of nonadherence to treatment crossed the U.S.-Mexico border approximately 20 times during April and May 2007. HHS and DHS worked together to try to prevent him from crossing the border, but attempts to identify him in DHS databases failed on several occasions. According to HHS officials, both individuals were eventually located and received treatment, and none of the people who might have been in contact with these individuals were reported to have contracted TB." (U.S. Government Accountability Office, Public Health and Border Security: HHS and DHS Should Further Strengthen Their Ability to Respond to TB Incidents, GAO-09-58, October 2008, p. 2-3).

[27] Centers for Disease Control and Prevention, "Trends in Tuberculosis—United States, 2013," MMWR, vol. 63, no. 11, March 21, 2014, pp. 229-233, http://www.cdc.gov /mmwr/ pdf/ wk/mm6311.pdf.

[28] Ibid.

[29] U.S. Department of State Bureau of Consular Affairs, Frequently Asked Questions—Immigrant Visa Interview Medical Examination, http://travel.state.gov/visa/immigrants /info/ info_3745.html#_What_should_the.

[30] INA §222(f) provides that if an immigrant visa is not issued, all medical eligibility forms will be treated as confidential.

[31] 9 FAM §40.11 N.5.2.

[32] The text actually names the Attorney General, but the passage of the Homeland Security Act of 2002 transferred the waiver power to the Secretary of Homeland Security.
[33] INA §212(g), 8 U.S.C. §1182(g).
[34] INA §212(g)(1), 8 U.S.C. §1182(g)(1).
[35] INA §212(g)(2), 8 U.S.C. §1182(g)(2).
[36] INA §212(g)(3). 8 U.S.C. §1182(g)(3).
[37] INA, §212(d)(13)(B)(i).
[38] CRS analysis of Table XX, Report of the Visa Office, U.S. Department of State, Bureau of Consular Affairs (FY2013), http://travel.state.gov/content/visas/english/law-and-policy/statistics.html.
[39] CRS analysis of Table XX, Report of the Visa Office, U.S. Department of State, Bureau of Consular Affairs (FY2013), http://travel.state.gov/content/visas/english/law-and-policy/statistics.html.
[40] INA §212(a)(ii).
[41] Ibid.
[42] See CDC Immigration Requirements: Technical Instructions for Vaccination, Table 1 (2007). On April 8, 2009, the CDC issued a notice with comment period that minor modifications would be made to the vaccination requirements under the Immigration and Nationality Act. For more information, see Centers for Disease Control and Prevention, Department of Health and Human Services, "Criteria for Vaccination Requirements for U.S. Immigration Purposes," 74 Federal Register 15986-15987, April 8, 2009.
[43] U.S. Department of State Bureau of Consular Affairs, 2008 Report of the Visa Office, Washington , DC, 2009, Appendix Table XX.
[44] INA §212(g)(2).
[45] For a complete listing of the ports of entry, see http://www.cbp.gov/contact/ports.
[46] CRS Report R43356, Border Security: Immigration Inspections at Ports of Entry, by Lisa Seghetti.
[47] See CDC, Division of Global Migration and Quarantine, http://www.cdc. gov/ ncezid/ dgmq/. In addition to non-regulatory activities, DGMQ has regulatory authority to prevent the introduction, transmission, and interstate spread of communicable diseases into the United States and its territories.
[48] Through an interagency agreement between the Department of Health and Human Services and the Department of Homeland Security, the Division of Immigration Health Services (DIHS) provides healthcare to undocumented migrants in the custody of Immigration and Customs Enforcement (ICE) residing in Service Processing Centers (SPC) and Contract Detention Facilities (CDF). DIHS, however, plays virtually no role in regard to inspection of travelers or screening of legal immigrants and nonimmigrants. For more information on DIHS, see archived CRS Report RL34556, Health Care for Noncitizens in Immigration Detention, by Alison Siskin.
[49] U.S. Department of Homeland Security, Inspector's Field Manual, Chapter 17, Section 9, Washington, DC, March 2006.
[50] Ibid.
[51] U.S. Government Accountability Office, Public Health and Border Security: HHS and DHS Should Further Strengthen Their Ability to Respond to TB Incidents, GAO-09-58, October 2008, pp. 49-50.
[52] TECS II is a computerized information system designed to identify suspected violators of federal law, as well as a communications system permitting message transmittal between certain federal, national, state, and local law enforcement agencies. Immigration inspectors

use the Interagency Border Inspections System (IBIS) at ports of entry to verify and obtain information on aliens presenting themselves for entry into the United States. IBIS is a broad system that sits on TECS II and interfaces with other databases as well. Because of the numerous systems and databases that interface with IBIS, the system is able to obtain such information as whether an alien is admissible, an alien's criminal information, and whether an alien is wanted by law enforcement.

[53] Ibid. If the incident occurs at a port of entry collocated with a quarantine station, CBP officials are instructed to notify the CDC official at the quarantine station on-site. However, all ports of entry have access to on-call medical personnel.

[54] CDC have issued guidelines for airlines that detail the necessary precautions and infection control procedures the airline personnel should follow. Centers for Disease Control, Interim Guidance about Ebola Infection for Airline Crews, Cleaning Personnel, and Cargo Personnel, Ebola Guidance for Airlines, August 11, 2014, http://www.cdc.gov/quarantine/air/managing-sick-travelers/ebola-guidance-airlines.html.

[55] Centers for Disease Control, "Press Briefing Transcript, CDC Telebriefing on Ebola outbreak in West Africa," press release, July 28, 2014, http://www.cdc.gov/ media/releases/2014/t0728-ebola.html.

[56] CRS Report IN10126, Safe at Home? Letting Ebola-Stricken Americans Return, by Sarah A. Lister.

[57] U.S. Department of Health and Human Services Centers for Disease Control, Technical Instructions for Medical Examination of Aliens, June 12, 1991, as revised in July 1992; including the Addendum to the Technical Instructions for Medical Examination of Alien, added October 6, 2008.

In: Removal and Exclusion of Foreign Nationals ISBN: 978-1-63482-610-5
Editor: Delia Gibson

Chapter 3

IMMIGRATION: TERRORIST GROUNDS FOR EXCLUSION AND REMOVAL OF ALIENS*

Michael John Garcia and Ruth Ellen Wasem

SUMMARY

The Immigration and Nationality Act (INA) spells out a strict set of admissions criteria and exclusion rules for all foreign nationals who come permanently to the United States as immigrants (i.e., legal permanent residents) or temporarily as nonimmigrants. Notably, any alien who engages in terrorist activity, or is a representative or member of a designated foreign terrorist organization, is generally inadmissible. After the September 11, 2001, terrorist attacks, the INA was broadened to deny entry to representatives of groups that endorse terrorism, prominent individuals who endorse terrorism, and (in certain circumstances) the spouses and children of aliens who are removable on terrorism grounds. The INA also contains grounds for inadmissibility based on foreign policy concerns.

The report of the National Commission on Terrorist Attacks Upon the United States (also known as the 9/11 Commission) concluded that the key officials responsible for determining alien admissions (consular officers abroad and immigration inspectors in the United States) were not considered full partners in counterterrorism efforts prior to September 11, 2001, and as a result, opportunities to intercept the September 11

* This is an edited, reformatted and augmented version of a Congressional Research Service report, RL32564, dated January 12, 2010.

terrorists were missed. The 9/11 Commission's monograph, *9/11 and Terrorist Travel*, underscored the importance of the border security functions of immigration law and policy.

In the 110th Congress, legislation was enacted to modify the terrorism-related grounds for inadmissibility and removal, as well as the impact that these grounds have upon alien eligibility for relief from removal. The Consolidated Appropriations Act, 2008 (P.L. 110-161) modified certain terrorism-related provisions of the INA, including exempting specified groups from the INA's definition of "terrorist organization" and expanding immigration authorities' waiver authority over the terrorism-related grounds for exclusion. P.L. 110-257 expressly excludes the African National Congress (ANC) from being considered a terrorist organization, and provides immigration authorities the ability to exempt most terrorism-related and criminal grounds for inadmissibility from applying to aliens with respect to activities undertaken in opposition to apartheid rule in South Africa. Immigration reform is an issue in the 111th Congress, and legislative proposals may contain provisions modifying the immigration consequences of terrorism-related activity.

The case of Umar Farouk Abdulmutallab, who allegedly attempted to ignite an explosive device on Northwest Airlines Flight 253 on December 25, 2009, has refocused attention on terrorist screening during the visa process. He was traveling on a multi-year, multiple-entry tourist visa issued to him in June 2008. State Department officials have acknowledged that Abdulmutallab's father came into the Embassy in Abuja, Nigeria, on November 19, 2009, to express his concerns about his son, and that those officials at the Embassy in Abuja sent a cable to the National Counterterrorism Center. State Department officials maintain they had insufficient information to revoke his visa at that time.

INTRODUCTION

In the years following the September 11, 2001, terrorist attacks, considerable concern has been raised because the 19 terrorists were aliens (i.e., foreign nationals) who apparently entered the United States on temporary visas despite provisions in immigration law intended to bar the admission of suspected terrorists. The report of the National Commission on Terrorist Attacks Upon the United States (also known as the 9/11 Commission) contended that "[t]here were opportunities for intelligence and law enforcement to exploit al Qaeda's travel vulnerabilities." The 9/11 Commission maintained that border security was not considered a national security matter prior to September 11, and as a result the consular and immigration officers were not treated as full partners in counterterrorism efforts.[1] The 9/11 Commission's monograph, *9/11 and Terrorist Travel*, underscored the importance of the border security functions of immigration law and policy.[2]

In the 108th Congress, several proposals were introduced in response to the 9/11 Commission's findings, some of which contained provisions relating to border security,[3] most notably the Intelligence Reform and Terrorism Prevention Act of 2004 (P.L. 108-458). In the 109th Congress, the REAL ID Act of 2005 (P.L. 109-13, Division B) included, among other things, a number of provisions related to immigration reform and document security that were considered during congressional deliberations on the Intelligence Reform and Terrorism Prevention Act, but which were ultimately not included.[4]

Under current law, three departments—the Department of State (DOS), the Department of Homeland Security (DHS) and the Department of Justice (DOJ)—play key roles in administering the law and policies on the admission of aliens.[5] DOS's Bureau of Consular Affairs (Consular Affairs) is the agency responsible for issuing visas, DHS's Citizenship and Immigration Services (USCIS) is charged with approving immigrant petitions, and DHS's Bureau of Customs and Border Protection (CBP) is tasked with inspecting all people who enter the United States. DOJ's Executive Office for Immigration Review (EOIR) has a significant policy role through its adjudicatory decisions on specific immigration cases.

This report focuses on the terrorism-related grounds for inadmissibility and deportation/removal. It opens with an overview of the terror-related grounds as they evolved through key legislation enacted in recent years. The section on current law explains the legal definitions of "terrorist activity," "engage in terrorist activity," and "terrorist organization," and describes the terror-related grounds for inadmissibility and removal. The report then discusses the alien screening process to determine admissibility and to identify possible terrorists, both during the visa issuance process abroad and the inspections process at US ports of entry.

Overview of Terrorist Exclusion

Grounds for Inadmissibility

With certain exceptions,[6] aliens seeking admission to the United States must undergo separate reviews performed by DOS consular officers abroad and CBP inspectors upon entry to the United States.[7] These reviews are intended to ensure that applicants are not ineligible for visas or admission under the grounds for inadmissibility spelled out in the Immigration and Nationality Act (INA).[8] These criteria are

- health-related grounds;
- criminal history;[9]
- security and terrorist concerns;
- public charge (e.g., indigence);
- seeking to work without proper labor certification;
- illegal entry and immigration law violations;
- ineligible for citizenship; and
- aliens previously removed.

Some grounds for inadmissibility may be waived or are not applicable in the case of nonimmigrants, refugees (e.g., public charge),[10] and other aliens. For aliens seeking to enter temporarily as nonimmigrants, even terrorism grounds for inadmissibility may possibly be waived.[11] As the terrorism grounds for inadmissibility have expanded to cover a broader range of activities and associations, some have believed it appropriate to ensure that immigration authorities are permitted to waive their application in certain circumstances.[12]

Key Legislation

Prior to the Immigration Act of 1990 (P.L. 101-649), there was no express terrorism-related ground for exclusion. Congress added the terrorism ground in the 1990 Act as part of a broader effort to streamline and modernize the security and foreign policy grounds for inadmissibility and removal. Before 1990, certain terrorists were excludable under security grounds, but the 1990 Act opened the door for broader elaboration of what associations and promotional activities could be deemed to be terrorist activities. In part as a response to the 1993 World Trade Center bombing, Congress strengthened the anti-terrorism provisions in the INA and passed provisions that many maintained would ramp up enforcement activities, notably in the Illegal Immigration Reform and Immigrant Responsibility Act (IIRIRA) of 1996 (P.L. 104-208) and the Antiterrorism and Effective Death Penalty Act (P.L. 104-132). As part of the Violent Crime Control Act of 1994 (P.L. 103-322),

Congress also amended the INA to establish temporary authority for an "S" nonimmigrant visa category for aliens who are witnesses and informants on criminal and terrorist activities. In September 2001, Congress enacted S. 1424 (P.L. 107-45), providing permanent authority for admission under the S visa.

Enacted in October 2001, the USA PATRIOT Act (P.L. 107-56) was a broad anti-terrorism measure that included several important changes to immigration law. Specifically in the context of this report, the USA PATRIOT Act amended the INA to add more terrorism-related grounds for inadmissibility and expand the definitional scope of terms used to describe terrorism-related activities and organizations.

The Enhanced Border Security and Visa Entry Reform Act of 2002 (P.L. 107-173) aimed to improve the visa issuance process abroad as well as immigration inspections at the border. It expressly required the development of an interoperable electronic data system to share information relevant to alien admissibility and removability and the implementation of an integrated entry-exit data system. It also required that, beginning in October 2004, all newly issued visas have biometric identifiers. In addition to increasing consular officers' access to electronic information needed for alien screening, it expanded the training requirements for consular officers who issue visas.[13]

The Intelligence Reform and Terrorism Prevention Act of 2004 (P.L. 108-458) focused primarily on targeting terrorist travel through an intelligence and security strategy based on reliable identification systems and effective, integrated information-sharing. Its immigration provisions aimed at closer monitoring of persons entering and leaving the United States as well as tightening up the grounds for removal. It also authorized a substantial increase in funding for immigration-related homeland security.

The REAL ID Act (P.L. 109-13, Division B) represented a continuation in the trend to expand the terror-related grounds for exclusion and removal. Of particular relevance to this report, the REAL ID Act expanded the terror-related grounds for inadmissibility and deportability, and amended the definitions of "terrorist organization" and "engage in terrorist activity" used by the INA.

The Consolidated Appropriations Act, 2008 (P.L. 110-161), subsequently modified the application of certain terrorism-related provisions of the INA, including exempting 10 organizations from falling under the definition of "terrorist organization" and expanding immigration authorities' waiver authority over many terrorism-related INA provisions.

CURRENT LAW

Since 1990, certain "terrorism"-related activities by an alien have expressly been grounds for exclusion and removal. Over the years, these grounds have been expanded to expressly cover membership in terrorist organizations, as well as an increasingly broad range of activities in support of terrorism-related activities or entities. Many of the terrorism-related grounds for inadmissibility and deportation use certain terms—i.e., "terrorist activity," "engage in terrorist activity," and "terrorist organization"—that are expressly defined by the INA to describe particular kinds of conduct or entities. The following sections provide an overview of the terrorism-related terms defined by the INA, as well as the terrorism-related grounds for inadmissibility and deportation.

Definitions of Terror-Related Terms in the INA

Terms including "terrorist activity," "engage in terrorist activity," and "terrorist organization" are specifically defined for INA purposes and refer to distinct concepts. As these definitions change, so too does the scope of INA provisions that use them. The term "terrorist activity" refers to certain, specified acts of violence—for example, hijacking an airplane or assassinating a Head of State. "Engaging in terrorist activity" includes both the commission of direct acts of terrorism and certain activities in support of them, such as soliciting participation in a terrorist act. The INA defines "terrorist organization" to include two general categories of groups. The first category includes groups that have been designated as terrorist organizations by the United States, thereby providing public notice of these organizations' involvement in terrorism. The second category includes other groups that carry out terror-related activities, but have not been designated either because they are operating under the radar or have shifting alliances, or because designating the group as a terrorist organization would jeopardize ongoing US criminal or military operations. The groups belonging to this second category may be called non-designated terrorist organizations.

The terms "engage in terrorist activity" and "terrorist organization" were amended by the REAL ID Act to cast a wider net over groups and persons who provide more discrete forms of assistance to terrorist organizations, particularly with respect to fund-raising and soliciting membership in those organizations. Subsequently, the Consolidated Appropriations Act FY2008 expressly exempted certain groups from being considered "terrorist organizations" and authorized immigration authorities to exempt other groups from being considered "terrorist organizations" when certain criteria were met. The act also specified the Taliban as a "terrorist organization" for INA purposes.

Definition of "Terrorist Activity" under the INA

"Terrorist activity" is defined by INA § 212(a)(3)(B)(iii). In order for an action to constitute "terrorist activity," it must have been unlawful in the place where it was committed (or, if it would have occurred in the United States, have been unlawful under US law) and involve

- the hijacking or sabotage of an aircraft, vessel, or other vehicle;
- seizing or detaining, and threatening to kill, injure, or continue to detain, another individual in order to compel a third person (including a governmental organization) to do or abstain from doing any act as an explicit or implicit condition for the release of the individual seized or detained;
- a violent attack upon an internationally protected person (e.g., Head of State, Foreign Minister, or ambassador);[14]
- an assassination;
- the use of any biological agent, chemical agent, or nuclear weapon or device;
- the use of any explosive, firearm, or other weapon or dangerous device (*other than for mere personal monetary gain*), with intent to endanger, directly or indirectly, the safety of one or more individuals or to cause substantial damage to property;[15] or
- a threat, attempt, or conspiracy to commit any of the foregoing.

Definition of "Terrorist Organization" under the INA

The REAL ID Act expanded the INA's definition of "terrorist organization" to include a broader range of groups that provide indirect assistance to other groups involved in terrorist activities. Further, the INA's definition of "terrorist organization" now covers entities that have not directly engaged in terrorist activities or assisted terrorist organizations, but have *subgroups* that do so. For purposes of the INA, a "terrorist organization" may describe groups falling into one of three categories ("Tiers"):

- any group designated by the Secretary of State as a terrorist organization pursuant to INA § 219, on account of that entity threatening the security of US nationals or the national security of the United States ("Tier I");
- upon publication in the *Federal Register*, any group designated as a terrorist organization by the Secretary of State in consultation with or upon the request of the Attorney General or Secretary of Homeland Security, after finding that the organization engages in terrorist activity ("Tier II"); and
- any group of two or more individuals, whether organized or not, which engages in, or has a subgroup that engages in terrorist activity ("Tier III").[16]

The Consolidated Appropriations Act, 2008, specifies that the Taliban is considered a Tier I terrorist organization.[17]

Waiver of Application and Inapplicability of "Terrorist Organization" Definition to Members of Certain Groups

The definition of "terrorist organization" is quite broad, potentially covering any group that either directly engages or has a subgroup that engages in terrorist activity, regardless of whether the group has actually been designated by US authorities as "terrorist." Possibly complicating matters further is that the INA defines "terrorist activity" and "engage[ing] in terrorist activity" broadly, arguably ignoring the context in which activity occurs and whether such activity is supported by the United States. For example, the use of weapons to endanger the safety of persons or cause substantial damage to property (other than for monetary gain) is considered "terrorist activity." Accordingly, a pro-democracy group engaged in armed conflict against an oppressive regime could potentially be considered a "terrorist organization" under the INA, even if the group's activities were supported by the United States, and as a result the persons involved with the group could be inadmissible and ineligible for asylum.[18]

Prior to the enactment of the Consolidated Appropriations Act, 2008, the Secretary of State or Secretary of Homeland Security, following consultation with the other and the Attorney General, had authority to waive the application of this provision with respect to a group that might otherwise constitute a "terrorist organization" solely on account of having a *subgroup* that had engaged in terrorist activity.[19] However, US authorities could *not* waive the application of this provision with respect to any group that had itself "engage[d] in terrorist activity."[20] Some policymakers expressed concern over the consequences of the limited scope of this waiver authority. In a September 2006 congressional hearing, a State Department representative testified that

> Although Secretarial exercise of the inapplicability authority allows us to make significant progress in reaching some populations in need of resettlement, it does not provide the flexibility required in all refugee cases. For example, Cuban anti-Castro freedom fighters and Vietnamese Montagnards who fought alongside US forces have been found inadmissible on this basis, as have Karen who participated in resistance to brutal attacks on their families and friends by the Burmese regime. The Administration will continue to seek solutions for these groups and to further harmonize national security concerns with the refugee admissions program.[21]

The Consolidated Appropriations Act, 2008, amended the INA to permit appropriate immigration authorities to waive application of the INA's "terrorist organization" definition to any non-designated (i.e., Tier III) group, except when the group has either engaged in terrorist activity against the United States or another democratic country, or purposefully engaged in a pattern of terrorist activity against civilians.[22]

On the basis of activities occurring before the act's date of enactment, section 691(b) of the Consolidated Appropriations Act, Division J, further specified that 10 groups are not considered "terrorist organizations" for INA purposes. These groups are

- the Karen National Union/Karen National Liberation Army (KNU/KNLA);
- the Chin National Front/Chin National Army (CNF/CNA);
- the Chin National League for Democracy (CNLD);
- the Kayan New Land Party (KNLP);
- the Arakan Liberation Party (ALP);
- the Tibetan Mustangs;
- the Cuban Alzados;
- the Karenni National Progressive Party (KNPP);
- appropriate groups affiliated with the Hmong; [23] and
- appropriate groups[24] affiliated with the Montagnards.

Immigration authorities had previously waived the application of the INA's "material support" provision to persons who provided *assistance* to all of the above-listed groups except the Hmong and Montagnards. Until enactment of the Consolidated Appropriations Act, however, *members* of these organizations could have faced immigration consequences on account of belonging to groups considered "terrorist organizations."

P.L. 110-257, which was enacted into law on July 1, 2008, retroactively amended the Consolidated Appropriations Act to include the African National Congress (ANC) among the list of groups not considered "terrorist organizations" for INA purposes.

Definition of "Engage in Terrorist Activity" under the INA

As discussed previously, the INA treats being "engaged in terrorist activity" as a separate concept from "terrorist activity" itself. The REAL ID Act amended the definition of "engage in terrorist activity" to cover more indirect forms of support for non-designated terrorist organizations. In order to "engage in terrorist activity," an alien must, either in an individual capacity or as part of an organization,[25]

- commit or incite to commit, under circumstances indicating an intention to cause death or serious bodily injury, a terrorist activity;
- prepare or plan a terrorist activity;
- gather information on potential targets for terrorist activity;
- solicit funds or other things of value for (1) terrorist activity, (2) a designated terrorist organization (i.e., a Tier I or Tier II organization), or (3) a non-designated terrorist organization (i.e., a Tier III organization), unless the solicitor can prove by clear and convincing evidence that he did not know, and should not have reasonably known, that the organization was a terrorist organization;
- solicit another individual to (1) engage in terrorist activity, (2) join a designated terrorist organization, or (3) join a non-designated terrorist organization, unless the solicitor can prove by clear and convincing evidence that he did not know, and should not have reasonably known, that the organization was a terrorist organization; or
- commit an act that the individual knows, or reasonably should know, provides material support to (1) the commission of a terrorist activity, (2) an individual or organization that the individual knows or should reasonably know has committed or plans to commit a terrorist activity, (3) a designated terrorist organization or member of such an organization, or (4) a non-designated terrorist organization or a member of such an organization, unless the actor can demonstrate by clear and convincing evidence that the actor did not know, and should

not reasonably have known, that the organization was a terrorist organization.[26]

Waiver of Application of Material Support Provision of "Engage in Terrorist Activity" Definition

Prior to the enactment of the Consolidated Appropriations Act, 2008, the INA included a provision, found at INA § 212(d)(3)(B), permitting immigration authorities to waive the application of the material support provision of the INA's "engage in terrorist activity" definition. Under prior law, an alien who provided material support to an individual or organization engaging in terrorist activity would not himself be considered to have "engaged in terrorist activity" for purposes of the INA if the Secretary of State or Secretary of Homeland Security, following consultation with the other and the Attorney General, concluded in his sole, unreviewable discretion that the definition of "engage in terrorist activity" did not apply with respect to the alien's material support.[27]

This waiver authority was used by the State Department and DHS to permit the consideration of applications for refugee status from aliens abroad and to consider asylum and adjustment of status claims for certain aliens present in the United States who provided material support to terrorist entities.[28] In 2006, the State Department waived the material support provision with respect to three large groups of refugees.[29] In 2007, DHS exercised waiver authority over the material support provision with respect to aliens who gave material support to one of the following eight groups:

- Karen National Union/Karen National Liberation Army (KNU/KNLA);
- Chin National Front/Chin National Army (CNF/CNA);
- Chin National League for Democracy (CNLD);
- Kayan New Land Party (KNLP);
- Arakan Liberation Party (ALP);
- Tibetan Mustangs;
- Cuban Alzados; or
- Karenni National Progressive Party (KNPP).[30]

This waiver applied only to aliens who provided material support to these organizations, not to aliens who were members of these groups. As previously discussed, the Consolidated Appropriations Act, 2008, enacted after the issuance of these waivers, specified that the above-listed groups would not be considered "terrorist organizations" for INA purposes. Accordingly, a person who provided material support to such groups would not be considered to have "engage[d] in terrorist activity," regardless of the Secretary of Homeland Security's prior decision to waive application of this provision.

The material support provision had been interpreted by immigration authorities as generally covering any support given to a terrorist entity, regardless of whether such support was provided due to duress or coercion.[31] DHS had opted not to apply the material support provision to persons who provided material support under duress to a terrorist organization, if a totality of the circumstances was deemed to justify the exemption.[32] In September 2007, the Secretary of Homeland Security exempted from the material support provision certain persons who provided material support under duress to the Revolutionary Armed Forces of Colombia (FARC).[33] In December 2007, DHS issued a similar exemption with respect to persons who provided material support under duress to the National Liberation Army of Columbia (ELN).[34]

The Consolidated Appropriations Act, 2008, replaced this waiver provision with a more general provision, discussed *infra* at "Waiver Authority over Inadmissibility Provisions." In June 2008, the Secretary of State and the Secretary of Homeland Security exercised waiver authority under INA § 212(d)(3)(B) with respect to aliens associated or affiliated with any of the 10 groups expressly exempted by the Consolidated Appropriations Act from being considered "terrorist organizations" for immigration purposes who were not otherwise granted relief under that exemption,[35] so long as certain criteria are fulfilled. Among other things, the waiver does not apply to aliens whose terrorist activities targeted non-combatants or aliens who pose a danger to the safety and security of the United States.[36]

Terrorism-Related Grounds for Inadmissibility or Deportation under Immigration Law

Engaging in specified, terrorism-related activity has direct consequences concerning an alien's ability to lawfully enter or remain in the United States. The INA provides that aliens engaged in terrorism-related activities generally cannot legally enter the United States. If an alien is legally admitted into the United States and subsequently engages in terrorist activity, he is deportable. Even if an alien does not fall under terrorism-related categories making him inadmissible or deportable, he might still be denied entry or removed from the United States on separate, security-related grounds.

Grounds for Inadmissibility and Deportation

The INA categorizes certain classes of aliens as inadmissible, making them "ineligible to receive visas and ineligible to be admitted to the United States."[37] Most recently, these grounds were expanded by the REAL ID Act in 2005, including by making activities such as espousal of terrorist activity and receipt of military-type training from or on behalf of a terrorist organization grounds for exclusion. The REAL ID Act also amended the terrorism-related grounds for deportability of aliens who have already entered the United States, so that these grounds are now the same as those for inadmissibility.[38] The terrorism-related grounds for inadmissibility and deportation are primarily found in INA §§ 212(a)(3)(B) and 237(a)(4)(B). An alien is inadmissible or deportable on terrorism-related grounds if he

- has engaged in a terrorist activity;
- is known or reasonably believed by a consular officer, the Attorney General, or the Secretary of Homeland Security to be engaged in or likely to engage in terrorist activity upon entry into the United States;
- has, under circumstances indicating an intention to cause death or serious bodily harm, incited terrorist activity;
- is a representative of (1) a designated or non-designated terrorist organization; or (2) any political, social, or other group that endorses or espouses terrorist activity;
- is a member of (1) any designated terrorist organization (i.e., a Tier I or Tier II organization); or (2) any non-designated terrorist organization (i.e., a Tier III organization), unless the alien can demonstrate by clear and convincing evidence that the alien did not know, and should not reasonably have known, that the organization was a terrorist organization;
- is an officer, official, representative, or spokesman of the Palestine Liberation Organization;[39]
- endorses or espouses terrorist activity or persuades others to endorse or espouse terrorist activity or support a terrorist organization;
- is the spouse or child of an alien who is inadmissible on terror-related grounds, if the activity causing the alien to be found inadmissible occurred within the last five years, unless the spouse or child (1) did not and should not have reasonably known about the terrorist activity or (2) in the reasonable belief of the consular officer or Attorney General, has renounced the activity causing the alien to be found inadmissible under this section;[40] or

- has received military-type training, from or on behalf of any organization that, at the time the training was received, was a terrorist organization.[41]

An additional, catch-all provision found at INA § 212(a)(3)(F) provides that association with terrorist organizations may also be grounds for inadmissibility. Any alien who either the Secretary of State or Attorney General, after consultation with the other, determines has been associated with a "terrorist organization and intends while in the United States to engage solely, principally, or incidentally in activities that could endanger the welfare, safety, or security of the United States," is inadmissible.[42] Pursuant to the REAL ID Act, this provision may also be used to remove an alien who has already been legally admitted into the United States.[43]

Waiver Authority over Inadmissibility Provisions

Prior to enactment of the Consolidated Appropriations Act FY2008, immigration authorities possessed exemption authority over the application of inadmissibility provisions concerning aliens who (1) were representatives of political, social, or other groups that endorse or espouse terrorist activity or (2) endorsed or espoused terrorist activity, or persuaded others to endorse or espouse terrorist activity or support a terrorist organization.[44] However, even prior to the enactment of the Consolidated Appropriations Act, immigration authorities possessed discretionary authority to waive application of the terrorism-related grounds for inadmissibility with respect to aliens seeking to temporarily enter the United States as non-immigrants.[45]

The Consolidated Appropriations Act FY2008 significantly broadened waiver authority over the terrorism-related grounds for inadmissibility. Now, the Secretary of State or Secretary of Homeland Security, in consultation with the other and the Attorney General, may generally waive application of almost all of the terrorism-related inadmissibility provisions contained in INA § 212(a)(3)(B).[46] However, only the Secretary of Homeland Security (not the Secretary of State) may exercise waiver authority with respect to an alien after removal proceedings against the alien are instituted.

Immigration authorities may *not* waive application of INA § 212(a)(3)(B) with respect to specified categories of aliens. These include aliens who

- are presently engaged or are likely to engage after entry in terrorist activity;
- voluntarily and knowingly engage or have engaged in terrorist activity on behalf of a designated (i.e., Tier I or Tier II) terrorist organization;

- voluntarily and knowingly have received military training from a Tier I or Tier II organization;
- are members or representatives of Tier I or Tier II organizations; or
- voluntarily and knowingly endorse or espouse the terrorist activity of a Tier I or Tier II organization, or convince others to support terrorist activity on behalf of a Tier I or Tier II organization.

While the Consolidated Appropriations Act generally expands immigration authorities' waiver authority, in contrast to prior law, the inadmissibility provision covering aliens who endorse or espouse terrorist activity may no longer be waived in situations where the endorsement or espousal of support concerned the terrorist activities of a Tier I or Tier II terrorist organization.

Although the Secretary of State and Secretary of Homeland Security are expressly accorded authority to waive certain terrorism-related grounds making an alien inadmissible under INA § 212, no similar waiver authority is expressly provided over the terror-related grounds that make an alien deportable under INA § 237, though language in the Consolidated Appropriations Act suggests that the waiver authority is intended to apply to both inadmissible and deportable aliens.[47]

Security-Related and Foreign Policy Grounds for Deeming an Alien Inadmissible

Even if an alien is not found inadmissible or deportable on terror-related grounds, he may nevertheless be removed from the United States or denied entry on separate, security-related grounds. An alien may be deemed inadmissible or deportable if he has engaged, is engaged, or (in the case of an alien not yet admitted into the United States) intends to engage in "any activity a purpose of which is the opposition to, or the control or overthrow of, the Government of the United States by force, violence, or other unlawful means."[48] In the case of aliens not yet admitted into the United States, either a consular officer or relevant immigration authority may designate an alien inadmissible if he has reasonable grounds to believe that the alien seeks to enter the United States to engage in such conduct.[49]

Further, if the Secretary of State has reasonable grounds to believe an alien's entry, presence, or activities in the United States would have potentially serious adverse foreign policy consequences for the United States, that alien may be deemed inadmissible or deportable.[50] However, aliens who are officials of foreign governments or purported foreign governments, or who are candidates for foreign office, are not inadmissible or deportable solely on account of their beliefs or statements.[51] Other aliens may not be deported or denied entry into the United States on account of their past, current, or expected beliefs, statements, or associations, if such beliefs, statements, or associations would be lawful within the United States, unless the Secretary of State personally determines that those aliens' admission would compromise a compelling United States foreign policy interest.[52] No similar limitation on removal is provided for aliens who are inadmissible or deportable on the separate, terrorism-related grounds concerning (1) espousal of terrorist activity or (2) association with a terrorist organization.

SCREENING ALIENS FOR ADMISSIBILITY

Visa Issuance

Personal interviews are required for all prospective legal permanent residents and are generally required for foreign nationals seeking nonimmigrant visas.[53] Pursuant to the Intelligence Reform and Terrorist Prevention Act of 2004, an in-person consular interview is required for most applicants between the ages of 14 and 79 for nonimmigrant visas. Consular officers use the Consular Consolidated Database (CCD) to screen visa applicants. Over 82 million records of visa applications are now automated in the CCD, with some records dating back to the mid-1990s.[54] Since February 2001, the CCD has stored photographs of all visa applicants in electronic form, and more recently the CCD has begun storing 10-finger scans. In addition to indicating the outcome of any prior visa application of the alien in the CCD, the system links with other databases to flag problems that may affect the issuance of the visa. The CCD is the nexus for screening aliens for admissibility, notably screening on terrorist security and criminal grounds.[55]

Terrorist Screening

For some years, consular officers have been required to check the background of all aliens in the "lookout" databases, specifically the Consular Lookout and Support System (CLASS). In 2003, Homeland Security Presidential Directive/HSPD-6 transferred certain terrorist watch list functions previously performed by the Department of State's Bureau of Intelligence and

Research to the Terrorist Screening Center (TSC), the entity that ultimately became the National Counterterrorism Center (NCTC).[56] NCTC has direct access to CCD and CLASS, as do the relevant DHS immigration and Department of Justice law enforcement agencies.[57]

The Security Advisory Opinion (SAO) system requires a consular officer abroad to refer selected visa cases for greater review by intelligence and law enforcement agencies.[58] The current interagency procedures for alerting officials about foreign nationals who may be suspected terrorists, referred to in State Department nomenclature as Visa Viper, began after the 1993 World Trade Center bombing and were institutionalized by enactment of the Enhanced Border Security and Visa Entry Reform Act of 2002. If consular officials receive information about a foreign national that causes concern, they send a Visa Viper cable (which is a dedicated and secure communication) to the NCTC. In 2009, consular posts sent approximately 3,000 Visa Viper communications to NCTC.[59]

In a similar set of SAO procedures, consular officers send suspect names, identified by law enforcement and intelligence information (originally certain visa applicants from 26 predominantly Muslim countries), to the FBI for a name check program called Visa Condor.[60] There is also the "Terrorist Exclusion List" (TEL), which lists organizations designated as terrorist-supporting and includes the names of individuals associated with these organizations.[61]

Controlled Technologies

With procedures distinct from the terrorist watch lists, consular officers screen visa applicants for employment or study that would give the foreign national access to controlled technologies, i.e., those that could be used to upgrade military capabilities, and refer foreign nationals from countries of concern (e.g., China, India, Iran, Iraq, North Korea, Pakistan, Sudan, and Syria) to the FBI and other key federal agencies.[62] This screening is part of a name-check procedure known as Visa Mantis, which has the following stated objectives: (1) stem the proliferation of weapons of mass destruction and missile delivery systems; (2) restrain the development of destabilizing conventional military capabilities in certain regions of the world; (3) prevent the transfer of arms and sensitive dual-use items to terrorist states; and (4) maintain US advantages in certain militarily critical technologies.

Biometric Visas

Aliens who are successful in their request for a visa are then issued the actual travel document.[63] Since October 2004, all visas issued by the United States use biometric identifiers (e.g., scans of the right and left index fingers) in addition to the digitized photograph that has been collected for some time.[64] These biometric data are available through the CCD, which links with the United States Visitor and Immigrant Status Indicator Technology (US-VISIT), DHS's automated entry and exit data system, at the time the visa is issued.

Terrorist Travel

The Intelligence Reform and Terrorist Prevention Act of 2004 established an Office of Visa and Passport Security in the Bureau of Diplomatic Security of the Department of State, headed by a person with the rank of Deputy Assistant Secretary of State for Diplomatic Security. The Deputy Assistant Secretary and appropriate Department of Homeland Security officials are tasked with preparing a strategic plan to target and disrupt individuals and organizations at home and in foreign countries that are involved in the fraudulent production, distribution, or use of visas, passports and other documents used to gain entry to the United States. This strategic plan is to emphasize individuals and organizations that may have links to domestic terrorist organizations or foreign terrorist organizations as defined by INA. The Office also analyzes methods used by terrorists to travel internationally, particularly the use of false or altered travel documents to illegally enter foreign countries and the United States, and it advises the Bureau of Consular Affairs on changes to the visa issuance process that could combat such methods, including the introduction of new technologies.

The Intelligence Reform and Terrorism Prevention Act of 2004 (P.L. 108-458) required the Secretary of DHS, in consultation with the Secretary of State, to submit to Congress a plan to ensure that DHS and DOS acquire and deploy to all consulates, ports of entry, and immigration services offices, technologies that facilitate document authentication and the detection of potential terrorist indicators on travel documents. The law further required that the plan address the feasibility of using such technologies to screen passports submitted for identification purposes to a United States consular, border, or immigration official.

By 2007, it appeared that DHS had not yet established the terrorist travel program mandated by §7215 of P.L. 108-458. As a consequence, §503 of the Implementing Recommendations of the 9/11 Commission Act of 2007 (P.L. 110-53) requires the Secretary to establish the program within 90 days of enactment and to report to Congress within 180 days on the implementation of the program. The act further requires that the Assistant Secretary for Policy at DHS (or another official that reports directly to the Secretary) be designated as head of the terrorist travel program and outlines specific duties to be carried out by the head of the program.

Admissibility at Ports of Entry

Border Inspections

The INA requires the inspection of all aliens who seek entry into the United States; possession of a visa or another form of travel document does not guarantee admission into the United States.[65] As a result, all persons seeking admission to the United States must demonstrate to a CBP inspector that they are a foreign national with a valid visa and/or passport or that they are a US citizen.[66] There are 327 official ports of entry in the United States, including 15 preclearance offices in Canada, Ireland, and the Caribbean. For FY2008, CBP reported inspecting approximately 409 million individuals (citizens as well as foreign nationals) at land, air, and sea ports of entry.[67] Because many foreign nationals are permitted to enter the United States without visas, notably, as discussed above, through the VWP, border inspections are extremely important for those having their initial screening at the port of entry.[68]

Primary inspection at the port of entry consists of a brief interview with a CBP officer, a cursory check of the traveler's documents and a query of the Interagency Border Inspection System (IBIS).[69] If the inspector is suspicious that the traveler may be inadmissible under the INA or in violation of other US laws, the traveler is referred to a secondary inspection. During secondary inspections, travelers are questioned extensively and travel documents are further examined. Several immigration databases are queried as well, including lookout databases.

US-VISIT

Under the US-VISIT system, certain foreign nationals are required to provide fingerprints, photographs or other biometric identifiers upon arrival in the United States. US-VISIT has grown from a photograph and two-finger biometric system for immigration identification[70] to the major identity management and screening system for DHS. CBP inspectors are currently taking a digital photograph and scanning 10 fingerprints from each foreign national who presents him or herself at designated ports of entry. According to DHS, US-VISIT operates and maintains two major automated identification systems in support of its mission: the Automated Biometric Identification System (IDENT) for biometric data, and the Arrival and Departure Information System (ADIS) for biographic data.[71]

Pre-Inspection

To keep inadmissible aliens from departing for the United States, IIRIRA required the implementation of a pre-inspection program at selected locations overseas. At these foreign airports, US immigration officers inspect aliens before their final departure to the United States. IIRIRA also authorized assistance to air carriers at selected foreign airports to help in the detection of fraudulent documents. The Intelligence Reform and Terrorist Prevention Act of 2004 directed DHS to expand the pre-inspection program at foreign airports to at least 15 and up to 25 airports, and submit a report on the progress of the expansion by June 30, 2006. The act also directed DHS to expand the Immigration Security Initiative, which places CBP inspectors at foreign airports to prevent people identified as national security threats from entering the country. The law required that at least 50 airports participate in the Immigration Security Initiative by December 31, 2006.

Expedited Removal under INA § 235(c)

Pursuant to INA § 235(c), in cases where the arriving alien is *suspected* of being inadmissible on security or related grounds, including terror-related activity, the alien may be summarily excluded by the regional director with no further administrative right to appeal. The Attorney General shall review such orders of removal.[72] If the Attorney General concludes on the basis of confidential information that the alien is inadmissible on security or related grounds under § 212(a)(3) of the INA, and determines after consulting with appropriate US security agencies that disclosure of such information would be prejudicial to the public interest, safety, or security, the regional director of the CBP is authorized to deny any further inquiry as to the alien's status and either order the alien removed or order disposal of the case as the director deems appropriate.[73]

Generally, an alien's removal to a particular country is withheld upon a showing that his life or freedom would be threatened in that country because of his race, religion, nationality, membership in a particular social group, or political opinion.[74] However, an alien is, with limited exception, ineligible for this remedy if, *inter alia*, he has been convicted of an aggravated felony or "there are reasonable grounds to believe that the alien is a danger to the security of the United States."[75] Pursuant to US legislation implementing the U.N. Convention against Torture and Other Cruel, Inhuman or Degrading Treatment or Punishment (CAT), all aliens—including those otherwise ineligible for withholding of removal and/or subject to expedited removal on security or related grounds such as terror-related activity—may not be removed to a country where they would more likely than not be tortured.[76]

LATEST LEGISLATIVE ACTIONS

Legislation was enacted in the 110th Congress to modify the terrorism-related grounds for inadmissibility and removal, as well as the impact that these grounds have upon alien eligibility for relief from removal. As previously discussed, the Consolidated Appropriations Act, 2008 (P.L. 110-161), enacted in December 2007, modified certain terrorism-related provisions of the INA, including by exempting specified groups from the INA's definition of "terrorist organization" and significantly expanding immigration authorities' waiver authority over the terrorism-related grounds for exclusion. P.L. 110-257, which was enacted into law on July 1, 2008, limits application of the terrorism-related grounds for inadmissibility with respect to the African National Congress (ANC) and certain ANC Members. Specifically, P.L. 110-257 expressly exempts the ANC from the INA's definition of "terrorist organization." The act also provides the Secretary of State and the Secretary of Homeland Security, in consultation with the other and the Attorney General, with authority to exempt most of the terrorism-related[77] and criminal grounds for inadmissibility from applying to aliens with respect to activities undertaken in opposition to apartheid rule in South Africa.[78] Further, federal authorities are required to take all necessary steps to ensure that databases used to determine admissibility to the United States are updated so that they are consistent with the exemptions provided to aliens for anti-apartheid activity. Immigration reform is an issue in the 111th Congress, and legislative proposals may contain provisions modifying the immigration consequences of terrorism-related activity.

Recent Concerns

Case of Umar Farouk Abdulmutallab

The case of Umar Farouk Abdulmutallab, who allegedly tried to take down Northwest Airlines Flight 253 on December 25, 2009, has refocused attention on terrorist screening during the visa issuance process. The 23-year-old Nigerian national allegedly tried unsuccessfully to ignite an explosive device on an incoming flight to Detroit. US consular officers in London, where Abdulmutallab was a student at University College London, had issued him a multi-year, multiple-visit tourist visa in June 2008. According to a State Department spokesman: "At the time that his visa was issued, there was nothing in his application nor in any database at the time that would indicate that he should not receive a visa. He was a student at a very reputable school. He had plenty of financial resources, so he was not an intending immigrant. There was no derogatory information about him last year—last June—that would indicate that he shouldn't get a visa, so we issued the visa."[79]

The suspect's father, a wealthy banker and former Nigerian government official, had reportedly contacted US officials to indicate his concern about his son's welfare and involvement in Islamic fanaticism. State Department officials have reported that the father came into the Embassy in Abuja, Nigeria, on November 19, 2009, to express his concerns about his son and that the consular officials at the Embassy in Abuja sent a cable to the National Counterterrorism Center (NCTC).[80] They relied on the standard interagency procedures for screening suspected terrorists, referred to as Visa Viper.[81] State Department officials acknowledge that a consular officer misspelled Abdulmutallab when conducting the name check in the CCD and as a result did not report in the Visa Viper that Abdulmutallab had received a visa in 2008. This error was reportedly corrected in a Visa Viper cable sent November 25, 2009.[82]

Visa Revocation

Some have questioned whether the Embassy in Abuja, Nigeria, or other US consular officials had sufficient authority and justification to revoke the visa issued to Abdulmutallab in London as a result of the information his father provided. According to a State Department spokesman: "[T]he information in this VISAS VIPER cable was insufficient for this interagency review process to make a determination that this individual's visa should be revoked."[83] While consular officers have the authority to issue and to revoke visas on terrorist grounds, they defer to the NCTC to identify suspected terrorists and designate known terrorists.[84]

After a visa has been issued, the consular officer as well as the Secretary of State has the discretionary authority to revoke a visa at any time.[85] A consular officer must revoke a visa if

- the alien is ineligible under INA §212(a) as described above to receive such a visa, or was issued a visa and overstayed the time limits of the visa;
- the alien is not entitled to the nonimmigrant visa classification under INA §101(a)(15) definitions specified in such visa;
- the visa has been physically removed from the passport in which it was issued; or
- the alien has been issued an immigrant visa.[86]

The Foreign Affairs Manual (FAM) instructs: "in making any new determination of ineligibility as a result of information which may come to light after issuance of a visa, the consular officer must seek and obtain any required advisory opinion." This applies, for example, to findings of ineligibility under "misrepresentation," "terrorist activity," or "foreign policy." FAM further instructs: "pending receipt of the Department's advisory opinion, the consular officer must enter the alien's name in the CLASS under a quasi-refusal code, if warranted."[87] According to DOS officials, they sometimes prudentially revoke visas (i.e., they revoke a visa as a safety precaution).[88] When a consular officer suspects that a visa revocation may involve US law enforcement interests, FAM instructs the consular officer to consult with law enforcement agencies at post and inform the State officials of the case, to permit consultations with potentially interested entities before a revocation is made.[89] The rationale for this consultation is that there may be legal or intelligence investigations that would be compromised if the visa were revoked and that law enforcement and intelligence officials may prefer to monitor the individual to further investigate his actions and associates.

Visa revocation has been a ground for removal in INA §237(a)(1)(B) since enactment of P.L. 108- 458 in December 2004. That provision (§5304 of P.L. 108-458) permits limited judicial review of removal if visa revocation is the sole basis of the removal.

End Notes

[1] National Commission on Terrorist Attacks Upon the United States, *The 9/11 Commission Report*, Executive Summary, at 14 (July 2004).

[2] National Commission on Terrorist Attacks Upon the United States, *9/11 and Terrorist Travel* (August 2004).

[3] For further analysis, see CRS Report RL32616, *9/11 Commission: Legislative Action Concerning US Immigration Law and Policy in the 108th Congress*, by Michael John Garcia and Ruth Ellen Wasem.

[4] For a detailed analysis of the REAL ID Act, see CRS Report RL32754, *Immigration: Analysis of the Major Provisions of the REAL ID Act of 2005*, by Michael John Garcia, Margaret Mikyung Lee, and Todd B. Tatelman.

[5] Other departments, notably the Department of Labor (DOL) and the Department of Agriculture (USDA), play roles in the approval process depending on the category or type of visa sought, and the Department of Health and Human Services (HHS) sets policy on the health-related grounds for inadmissibility.

[6] Certain classes of aliens are not required to obtain a visa to enter the United States and are therefore exempt from the consular review process. For example, under the visa waiver program (VWP), nationals from certain countries are permitted to enter the United States as temporary visitors (nonimmigrants) for business or pleasure without first obtaining a visa from a US consulate abroad. See INA § 217; 8 USC. § 1187. For additional background on the VWP, see CRS Report RL32221, *Visa Waiver Program*, by Alison Siskin.

[7] For background and analysis of alien screening and visa issuance policy, see CRS Report RL31512, *Visa Issuances: Policy, Issues, and Legislation*, by Ruth Ellen Wasem.

[8] INA § 212(a); 8 USC. § 1182(a).

[9] For a full discussion of this ground, see CRS Report RL32480, *Immigration Consequences of Criminal Activity*, by Yule Kim and Michael John Garcia.

[10] All family-based immigrants and employment-based immigrants who are sponsored by a relative must have binding affidavits of support signed by US sponsors in order to show that they will not become public charges.

[11] INA § 212(d)(3)(A); 8 USC. § 1182(d)(3)(A).

[12] *See, e.g.*, Consolidated Appropriations Act, 2008, P.L. 110-161, Div. J, § 691 (expanding waiver authority over terrorism-related grounds for inadmissibility); *International Terrorism: Threats and Responses, Hearings on H.R. 1710, the Comprehensive Antiterrorism Act of 1995, Before the House Comm. on the Judiciary* , 104th Cong., 1st Sess., 243-244 (1995) (testimony of Jamie S. Gorelick, Deputy Attorney General) (while strongly endorsing greater antiterrorism authority, also observing that it might be in the interest of the United States to allow a member of a terrorist organization to enter in some circumstances).

[13] CRS Report RS21438, *Immigration Legislation Enacted in the 107th Congress*, by Andorra Bruno.

[14] "Internationally protected person" is defined under US law as "(A) a Chief of State or the political equivalent, head of government, or Foreign Minister whenever such person is in a country other than his own and any member of his family accompanying him; or (B) any other representative, officer, employee, or agent of the United States government, a foreign government, or international organization who at the time and place concerned is entitled pursuant to international law to special protection against attack upon his person, freedom,

or dignity, and any member of his family then forming part of his household." 18 USC. § 1116(b)(4).

[15] In *McAllister v. Attorney General of the United States*, 444 F.3d 178 (3rd Cir. 2006), the Third Circuit Court of Appeals discussed some of the situations in which this provision would not apply: First, the parenthetical phrase "other than for mere personal monetary gain" removes common crimes from the definition by requiring that the offending activity be conducted for reasons other than money. For that reason, offenses like robbery and burglary are not included in the definition. Second, the *mens rea* element of the provision requires the actor to have the specific intent to endanger the safety of individuals or to cause substantial damage to property. Thus, the definition of terrorist activity does not include situations in which an alien has acted in self-defense or in which the alien lacks the capacity to meet the requisite intent. More importantly, none of the aforementioned activities constitute a protected activity outside of the permissible bounds of Congressional regulation. *Id.* at 186.

[16] INA § 212(a)(3)(B)(iv); 8 USC. § 1182(a)(3)(B)(iv). The USA PATRIOT ACT previously amended INA § 212 to expand the definition of "terrorist organization" to potentially include terrorist organizations not designated pursuant to INA § 219.

[17] P.L. 110-161, Div. J, § 691(d).

[18] *See* In re S-K-, 23 I. & N. Dec. 936, 941 (BIA 2006) ("Congress intentionally drafted the terrorist bars to relief very broadly, to include even those people described as 'freedom fighters,' and it did not intend to give us discretion to create exceptions for members of organizations to which our Government might be sympathetic."). *See also Khan v. Holder,* 584 F.3d 773, 784-785 (9th Cir. 2009) (endorsing the reasoning of the BIA in *In re S-K-*, and also holding that "the definition of 'terrorist activity' under the INA does not provide an exception for armed resistance against military targets that is permitted under the international law of armed conflict").

[19] This waiver provision was added by the REAL ID Act.

[20] INA § 212(a)(3)(B)(iii); 8 USC. § 1182(a)(3)(B)(iii) (2006).

[21] Senate Committee on the Judiciary, Subcommittee on Immigration, Border Security and Citizenship, *Hearing on Oversight of US Refugee Admissions and Policy*, 109th Cong., 2nd sess., September 27, 2006 (testimony of Ellen Sauerbrey, Asst. Sec.for the Bureau of Population, Refugees, and Migration).

[22] P.L. 110-161, Div. J, § 691(a).

[23] Immigration authorities have interpreted the phrase "appropriate groups," when applied to entities affiliated with the Hmong, to include "ethnic Hmong individuals or groups, provided that there is no reason to believe that the relevant activities of the recipients were targeted against noncombatants...." Memorandum from USCIS Acting Deputy Direct Michael L. Aytes, Implementation of section 691 of Division J of the Consolidated Appropriations Act, 2008, and Updated Processing Requirements for Discretionary Exemptions to Terrorist Activity Inadmissibility Grounds, Jul. 28, 2008, at 5, available at http://www.uscis.gov/files/nativedocuments/caa_691_28_july_08.pdf.

[24] Immigration authorities have interpreted the phrase "appropriate groups," when applied to entities affiliated with the Montagnards, to include the Front Unifié de Lutte des Races Opprimées (FULRO). *Id.*at 5.

[25] An alien can be found to have "engage[d] in terrorist activity" on account of activities taken on behalf of an organization, even if that group has not been deemed a "terrorist organization" for INA purposes. *McAllister*, 444 F.3d at 187 (determination that an alien had "engage[d] in terrorist activity" on account of actions taken as a member of the Irish National

Liberation Army (INLA) did not require a determination that the INLA was a "terrorist organization").

[26] INA § 212(a)(3)(B)(iv); 8 USC. § 1182(a)(3)(B)(iv).

[27] INA § 212(d)(3)(B); 8 USC. § 1182(d)(3)(B) (as amended by §104 of the REAL ID Act).

[28] *See* Dept. of Homeland Security, Press Release, *Statement by Homeland Security Secretary Michael Chertoff on the Intention to Use Discretionary Authority for Material Support to Terrorism*, January 19, 2007, *available at* http://www.dhs.gov/xnews/releases/pr_1169465766808.shtm. Aliens who are inadmissible or deportable on terrorism-related grounds are generally ineligible for asylum. INA § 208(b)(2)(A)(v); 8 USC. § 1158(b)(2)(A)(v).

[29] State Department Office of the Spokesman, Press Release, *The Department of State Decides Material Support Inapplicable to Chin Refugees from Burma*, October 19, 2006, *available at* http://www.state74761.htm.

[30] Exercise of Authority Under Sec. 212(d)(3)(B)(i) of the Immigration and Nationality Act, 72 Fed. Reg. 9954 (March 6, 2007).

[31] *See* Note, *Admission Denied: in Support of a Duress Exception to the Immigration and Nationality Act's "Material Support for Terrorism" Provision*, 20 GEO. IMMIGR. L.J. 437, 458-468 (2006) (discussing decisions by immigration judges interpreting the "material support" provision to cover support given under duress and coercion).

[32] Exercise of Authority Under Sec. 212(d)(3)(B)(i) of the Immigration and Nationality Act 72 Fed. Reg. 9958 (March 6, 2007) (concerning application of material support provision to Tier III organizations); Exercise of Authority Under Sec. 212(d)(3)(B)(i) of the Immigration and Nationality Act 72 Fed. Reg. 26138 (May 8, 2007) (concerning application of material support provision to Tier I and Tier II organizations).

[33] US Citizenship and Immigration Services, Fact Sheet, *USCIS Implements Authority to Exempt Certain Persons Who Provided Material Support under Duress to the Revolutionary Armed Forces of Colombia (FARC)*, September 26, 2007, *available online at* http://www.uscis.gov/files/pressrelease/MaterialSupportFS_26Sep07.pdf.

[34] Dept. of Homeland Security, Authorization Document, *Authorization to Process Cases Involving the Provision of Material Support to the ELN* (December 18, 2007).

[35] See *supra* at pg. 9.

[36] Exercise of Authority Under Sec. 212(d)(3)(B)(i) of the Immigration and Nationality Act, 73 Fed. Reg. 34770-34776 (June 18, 2008).

[37] INA § 212(a); 8 USC. § 1182(a).

[38] Prior to the enactment of the REAL ID Act, the terrorism-related grounds for deportation were significantly less broad than the terror-related grounds for inadmissibility. Previously, an alien was deportable on terror-related grounds only if he had engaged or was presently engaged in terrorist activity. INA § 237(a)(4)(B); 8 USC. § 1227(a)(4)(B) (2004). Membership in or association with a terrorist organization, the endorsement or espousal of terrorist activity, or being the spouse or child of an alien who was inadmissible to the United States on terror-related grounds did not provide grounds for deporting an alien legally present in the United States, even if such grounds would make an alien seeking to enter the United States statutorily inadmissible.

[39] "An alien who is an officer, official, representative, or spokesman of the Palestine Liberation Organization is considered, for purposes of this chapter, to be engaged in a terrorist activity." INA § 212(a)(3)(B), 8 USC. § 1182(a)(B).

[40] Due to an apparent drafting error, the exception to the inadmissibility ground concerning the spouse or child of an alien who is inadmissible on terrorism-related grounds did not cross-

reference the correct INA provision. *See* INA § 212(a)(3)(B)(ii); 8 USC. § 1182(a)(3)(B)(ii) (2006) (citing to INA § 212(a)(3)(B)(i)(VII), which concerns the inadmissibility of aliens who espouse or endorse terrorist activity, rather than INA § 212(a)(3)(B)(i)(IX), which generally makes inadmissible the spouse or child of an alien who is inadmissible on terrorism-related grounds). The Consolidated Appropriations Act FY2008 amended this provision to cross-reference the correct INA provision. P.L. 110-161, § 691(c).

[41] "Military-type training" is defined under 18 USC. § 2339D(c)(1).

[42] INA § 212(a)(3)(F); 8 USC. § 1182(a)(3)(F).

[43] INA § 237(a)(4)(B); 8 USC. § 1227(a)(4)(B).

[44] INA § 212(d)(3)(B); 8 USC. § 1182(d)(3)(B).

[45] INA § 212(d)(3)(A); 8 USC. § 1182(d)(3)(B).

[46] The waiver does not affect the application of INA § 212(a)(3)(F), which permits immigration authorities to exclude associates of terrorist organizations in certain circumstances.

[47] See P.L. 110-161, Div. J, § 691(f) (stating that INA §§ 212(a)(3)(B) and 212(d)(3)(B), as amended by the act, "shall apply to (1) removal proceedings instituted before, on, or after the date of enactment of this section; and (2) acts and conditions constituting a ground for inadmissibility, excludability, deportation, or removal occurring or existing before, on, or after such date").

[48] INA §§ 212(a)(3)(A), 237(a)(3)(A), 8 USC. §§ 1182(a)(3)(A), 1227(a)(3)(A).

[49] INA § 212(a)(3)(A); 8 USC. § 1182(a)(3)(A).

[50] INA § 212(a)(3)(C); 8 USC. § 1182(a)(3)(C).

[51] INA §§ 212(a)(3)(C)(ii), 237(a)(4)(C)(ii); 8 USC. §§ 1182(a)(3)(C)(ii), 1227(a)(4)(C)(ii).

[52] INA §§ 212(a)(3)(C)(iii), 237(a)(4)(C)(ii); 8 USC. §§ 1182(a)(3)(C)(iii), 1227(a)(4)(C)(ii).

[53] 22 C.F.R. § 42.62. Personal interview waivers may be granted only to children under age 14, persons 79 years or older, diplomats and representatives of international organizations, aliens who are renewing a visa they obtained within the prior 12 months, and individual cases for whom a waiver is warranted for national security or unusual circumstances. 22 C.F.R. § 41.102.

[54] According to the Department of State's Office of Legislative Affairs, consular officers have stored photographs of nonimmigrant visa applicants in an electronic database for over twelve years. These data are now in the CCD.

[55] For more on alien screening procedures and policy, see CRS Report RL31512, *Visa Issuances: Policy, Issues, and Legislation*, by Ruth Ellen Wasem.

[56] The White House, Homeland Security Presidential Directive/HSPD-6, *Subject: Integration and Use of Screening Information* (Washington, September 16, 2003). It ordered the creation of the Terrorist Screening Center (TSC) to consolidate terrorist watch lists. It was issued on September 16, 2003, and directed the operations to begin on December 1, 2003.

[57] Unclassified congressional staff briefing by Assistant Secretary of State Janice Jacobs, January 11, 2010. For background, see Testimony of Maura Harty, Assistant Secretary of State for Consular Affairs, National Commission on Terrorist Attacks Upon the United States, *US Government Agencies Aimed at Improving Border Security*, hearing, January 26, 2004.

[58] US Congress, Senate Committee on Foreign Relations, Subcommittee on International Operations and Terrorism, *The Post 9/11 Visa Reforms and New Technology: Achieving the Necessary Security Improvements in a Global Environment*, hearing, October 23, 2003.

[59] Unclassified congressional staff briefing by Assistant Secretary of State Janice Jacobs, January 11, 2010.

[60] US Congress, Senate Committee on Foreign Relations, Subcommittee on International Operations and Terrorism, *The Post 9/11 Visa Reforms and New Technology: Achieving the Necessary Security Improvements in a Global Environment*, hearing, October 23, 2003.

[61] For background and analysis, see CRS Report RL32120, *The "FTO List" and Congress: Sanctioning Designated Foreign Terrorist Organizations*, by Audrey Kurth Cronin.

[62] US General Accounting Office (now the US Government Accountability Office), *Export Controls: Department of Commerce Controls Over Transfers of Technology to Foreign Nationals Needs Improvement*, GAO-02-972 (September 2002).

[63] For a full discussion of biometric visas, see congressional distribution memorandum, *Biometric and Laser Visas: Background and Current Policy*, by Ruth Ellen Wasem, August 19, 2004.

[64] Section 414 of the USA PATRIOT ACT (P.L. 107-56) and Section 303 of the Enhanced Border Security and Visa Reform Act (P.L. 107-173) require that visas and other travel documents contain a biometric identifier and are tamper-resistant.

[65] CRS Report RL32399, *Border Security: Inspections Practices, Policies, and Issues*, by Ruth Ellen Wasem et al.

[66] CRS congressional distribution memorandum, *Western Hemisphere Travel Initiative*, by Ruth Wasem, Blas Nuñez-Neto, Susan Epstein, Todd Tatelman, and Angeles Villarreal, April 26, 2006.

[67] US Department of Homeland Security, *US Customs and Border Protection (CBP) Fiscal Year 2008 Performance and Accountability*, Washington, DC, February 2009.

[68] For further background, see CRS Report RS21899, *Border Security: Key Agencies and Their Missions*, by Chad C. Haddal.

[69] IBIS is a broad system that interfaces with the FBI's National Crime Information Center (NCIC), the Treasury Department's Enforcement and Communications System (TECS II), the former INS's National Automated Immigration Lookout System (NAILS) and Non-immigrant Information System (NIIS) and the DOS's Consular Consolidated Database (CCD), Consular Lookout And Support System (CLASS) and TIPOFF terrorist databases. Because of the numerous systems and databases that interface with IBIS, the system is able to obtain such information as whether an alien is admissible, an alien's criminal information, and whether an alien is wanted by law enforcement.

[70] DHS regulations exempted about 20 categories of individuals from providing biometric identifiers upon entry to or exit from the United States; however, the CBP inspector retains discretion to collect an alien's biometric information. CRS Report RL32234, *US Visitor and Immigrant Status Indicator Technology (US-VISIT) Program*, by Lisa M. Seghetti and Stephen R. Vina.

[71] US Department of Homeland Security, National Protection and Programs Directorate, *United States Visitor and Immigrant Status Indicator Technology, Fiscal Year 2010 Congressional Justification*, February 2009.

[72] INA § 235(c)(2)(A); 8 USC. § 1225(c)(2)(A).

[73] See 8 C.F.R. § 235.8(b)(1).

[74] INA § 241(b)(3); 8 USC. § 1231(b)(3).

[75] INA § 241(b)(3)(B); 8 USC. § 1231(b)(3)(B).

[76] Foreign Affairs Reform and Restructuring Act, P.L. 105-277, § 2242. For further discussion, see CRS Report RL32276, *The U.N. Convention Against Torture: Overview of US Implementation Policy Concerning the Removal of Aliens*, by Michael John Garcia.

[77] The act does not permit the exemption of INA § 212(a)(3)(B)(ii), which bars the admission of an alien who immigration authorities have reason to believe is currently engaged in or is likely to engage after entry in terrorist activity.

[78] The act also contains a provision expressing the sense of Congress that this provision should be used to exempt the anti-apartheid activities of aliens who are current or former officials of the government of the Republic of South Africa.

[79] Ian Kelly, *On-the-Record Briefing*, US Department of State, Washington , DC, December 28, 2009.

[80] Ian Kelly, *On-the-Record Briefing*, US Department of State, Washington , DC, December 28, 2009.

[81] For a more complete discussion of terrorist watch lists and the role of the National Counterterrorism Center, see CRS Report RL33645, *Terrorist Watchlist Checks and Air Passenger Prescreening*, by William J. Krouse and Bart Elias.

[82] Unclassified congressional staff briefing by Assistant Secretary of State Janice Jacobs, January 11, 2010.

[83] Ian Kelly, *On-the-Record Briefing*, US Department of State, Washington , DC, December 28, 2009.

[84] The White House, Homeland Security Presidential Directive/HSPD-6, *Subject: Integration and Use of Screening Information* (Washington, September 16, 2003). This directive transferred certain terrorist watch list functions previously performed by the Department of State's Bureau of Intelligence and Research to the entity that became the National Counterterrorism Center.

[85]INA § 221(i); 8 USC. §1201(i).

[86] 22 C.F.R. §41.122 Notes N1.

[87] 22 C.F.R. § 41.122 Notes PN3.

[88] Testimony of Janice L. Jacobs, Deputy Assistant Secretary of State for Visa Services, in US Congress, Senate Committee on the Judiciary, Subcommittee on Immigration, Border Security and Citizenship, *Visa Issuance, Information Sharing and Enforcement in a Post-9/11 Environment: Are We Ready Yet?* hearing, July 15, 2003.

[89] 22 C.F.R. § 41.122 Notes PN9.2-1.

In: Removal and Exclusion of Foreign Nationals ISBN: 978-1-63482-610-5
Editor: Delia Gibson

Chapter 4

IMMIGRATION CONSEQUENCES OF CRIMINAL ACTIVITY*

Yule Kim and Michael John Garcia

SUMMARY

Congress has broad plenary authority to determine classes of aliens who may be admitted into the United States and the grounds for which they may be removed. Pursuant to the Immigration and Nationality Act (INA), as amended, certain conduct may either disqualify an alien from entering the United States ("inadmissibility") or provide grounds for his or her removal/deportation. Prominently included among this conduct is criminal activity. "Criminal activity" comprises acts violative of federal, state, or, in many cases, foreign criminal law. It does *not* cover violations of the INA that are not crimes—most notably, being in the U.S. without legal permission. Thus, the term "illegal alien"—an alien without legal status—is not synonymous with "criminal alien."

Most crimes affecting immigration status are not specifically mentioned by the INA, but instead fall under a broad category of crimes, such as *crimes involving moral turpitude* or *aggravated felonies*. In addition, certain criminal conduct precludes a finding of *good moral character* under the INA, which is a requirement for naturalization and certain types of immigration relief.

---

* This is an edited, reformatted and augmented version of a Congressional Research Service publication, CRS Report for Congress, RL32480, from www.crs.gov, dated January 15, 2009.

In certain circumstances, grounds for inadmissibility or deportation may be waived. In some cases, aliens facing removal may be allowed to remain in the United States—for example, when they are granted discretionary or mandatory relief from removal for humanitarian reasons, such as through asylum, withholding of removal, or cancellation of removal. Aliens facing removal may also be permitted to depart the United States voluntarily, and thereby avoid the potential stigma and legal consequences of forced removal. Criminal conduct may affect an alien's eligibility for either voluntary departure or discretionary relief from removal. Additionally, criminal conduct is a key disqualifying factor under the character requirement for naturalization.

Several legislative proposals were made during the 110th Congress that contained provisions modifying the immigration consequences of criminal activity. Enacted legislation modifying the immigration consequences of criminal activity included P.L. 110-257, providing certain relief from inadmissibility to members of the African National Congress; P.L. 110-340, making persons who have engaged in the recruitment of child soldiers in violation of federal law inadmissible, deportable and ineligible for asylum or withholding of removal; and P.L. 110-457, modifying the grounds for inadmissibility and removal related to human trafficking.

INTRODUCTION

Congress has broad plenary authority to determine classes of aliens who may be admitted into the United States and the grounds for which they may be removed.[1] Pursuant to the Immigration and Nationality Act (INA),[2] as amended, certain conduct may either disqualify an alien from entering the United States or provide grounds for his or her removal. Prominently included among this conduct is criminal activity.

In general, aliens may legally enter the United States under one of three categories: (1) legal permanent residents (LPRs), who are also commonly referred to as immigrants; (2) nonimmigrants, who are aliens permitted to enter the United States temporarily for a specific purpose, such as for tourism, academic study, or temporary work; and (3) refugees, who are aliens facing persecution abroad and are of special humanitarian concern to the United States. There are two aspects for legal admission under each of these categories. First, an alien must fulfill the substantive requirements for admission under a specified category. For example, in order to enter the United States as a nonimmigrant student, an alien must demonstrate that he is a bona fide student at an approved school.[3] Second, aliens who fulfill substantive requirements for admission may nevertheless be denied admission if they fall within a class of inadmissable aliens listed under INA § 212.[4] Once admitted, aliens remain subject to removal if they fall within a class of deportable aliens listed under INA § 237.[5] The INA contains bars for admission and grounds for deportation based on criminal conduct.[6]

This report discusses the potential immigration consequences of criminal activity. "Criminal activity" generally refers to conduct for which an alien has been found or plead guilty before a court of law, though in limited circumstances consequences may attach to the *commission* of a crime or *admission of acts constituting the essential elements* of a crime. Consequences may flow from violations of either federal, state or, in many circumstances, foreign criminal law. Some federal crimes are set out in the INA itself—alien smuggling, for example. However, not all violations of immigration law are crimes. Notably, being in the U.S. without legal permission— i.e., being an "illegal alien"—is *not* a crime in and of itself.[7] Thus, for example, an alien who overstays a student visa may be an "illegal alien," in that the alien may be subject to removal from the U.S., but such an alien is not a "criminal alien."

Administration of Immigration Law

For several decades, the primary authority to interpret, implement, and enforce the provisions of the INA was vested with the Attorney General.[8] The Attorney General delegated most authority over immigration matters to two bodies within the Department of Justice (DOJ): the Immigration and Naturalization Service (INS), which was delegated authority over immigration enforcement and service functions, and the Executive Office of Immigration Review (EOIR), which was delegated adjudicatory functions over immigration matters. Following the establishment of the Department of Homeland Security (DHS), the INS was abolished and its functions were transferred to DHS. Pursuant to INA § 103(a)(1), as amended, the DHS Secretary is now "charged with the administration and enforcement of ... [the INA] and all other laws relating to the immigration and naturalization of aliens, except insofar as this chapter or such laws relate to the powers, functions, and duties conferred upon the ... [other executive officers and agencies including] the Attorney General.... "[9]

Pursuant to INA § 103, as amended, EOIR retains adjudicative authority over immigration matters, and rulings by the Attorney General with respect to questions of immigration law remain controlling upon immigration authorities.[10] However, the precise scope of the Attorney General's continued authority over other immigration matters remains unclear, because most provisions of the INA have not been specifically amended to reflect the transfer of certain immigration functions to DHS.[11] As a result, many of the regulations implemented by DHS and EOIR are presently duplicative or otherwise overlapping.[12] The Homeland Security Act of 2002, which established DHS and transferred to it many immigration functions previously conducted by the INS, provided a general guideline that immigration officials to whom immigration functions were transferred "may, for purposes of performing the function, exercise all authorities under any other provisions of law that were available with respect to the performance of that function to the official responsible for the performance of the function immediately before [transfer]."[13] As a practical matter, the DHS has primary day-to-day authority over immigration matters, while the Attorney General and EOIR maintain adjudicatory authority over immigration matters and questions of immigration law.

Categories of Criminal Aliens

The INA lists a number of criminal grounds for designating an alien as inadmissible or deportable. Most crimes included under these grounds are not specifically mentioned, but instead fall under a broad category of crimes, such as *crimes involving moral turpitude* or *aggravated felonies*. In addition, certain criminal conduct precludes a finding of *good moral character* under the INA, thereby preventing an alien from becoming either a naturalized U.S. citizen or a candidate for certain types of relief.

The class of *crimes involving moral turpitude*, the class of *aggravated felonies*, and the class of crimes that preclude a finding of *good moral character* are overlapping, but no two classes are coextensive. The types of crimes constituting *crimes of moral turpitude* are determined by case law. Crimes that are *aggravated felonies* are listed in statute, with case law illuminating the bounds of certain listed crimes. Crimes precluding a finding of *good moral character* are determined by a combination of case law and statutory law. These criminal classes are further modified for the purposes of specific INA provisions.[14] The following sections will describe these criminal categories in more detail.

Crimes Involving Moral Turpitude

Immigration law has used the term "moral turpitude" in its criminal grounds for exclusion since 1891.[15] Whether a crime involves moral turpitude has been determined by judicial and administrative case law rather than a statutory definition. In general, if a crime manifests an element of baseness or depravity under current mores—if it evidences an evil or predatory intent—it involves moral turpitude. Thus, certain crimes such as murder, rape, blackmail, and fraud have been considered crimes involving moral turpitude, whereas crimes such as simple assault have not been considered to involve moral turpitude.[16]

Aggravated Felonies

Since 1988, Congress has designated specific offenses as aggravated felonies for immigration purposes, and it has made removal of aliens convicted of such crimes a priority through streamlined procedures and ineligibility for various types of relief. Aggravated felonies were initially listed under the INA pursuant to the Anti-Drug Abuse Act of 1988[17] as part of a broad effort to combat narcotics trafficking. The only crimes designated in the 1988 Act were murder, drug trafficking, and illegal trafficking in firearms or destructive devices.[18] Subsequent legislation has expanded the definition of "aggravated felony" a number of times, to include certain categories of crimes and many specific crimes.

Section 101(a)(43) of the INA defines "aggravated felony" through the listing of a number of criminal categories and specified crimes. The broadest categories of aggravated felonies under the INA are as follows:

- any crime of violence (including crimes involving a substantial risk of the use of physical force) for which the term of imprisonment is at least one year;
- any crime of theft (including the receipt of stolen property) or burglary for which the term of imprisonment is at least one year; and
- illegal trafficking in drugs, firearms, or destructive devices.

Many specific crimes are also listed as aggravated felonies under the INA. These include the following:

- murder;
- rape;

- sexual abuse of a minor;
- illicit trafficking in a controlled substance, including a federal drug trafficking offense;
- illicit trafficking in a firearm, explosive, or destructive device;
- federal money laundering or engaging in monetary transactions in property derived from specific unlawful activity, if the amount of the funds exceeded $10,000;
- any of various federal firearms or explosives offenses;
- any of various federal offenses relating to a demand for, or receipt of, ransom;
- any of various federal offenses relating to child pornography;
- a federal racketeering offense;
- a federal gambling offense (including the transmission of wagering information in commerce if the offense is a second or subsequent offense) which is punishable by imprisonment of at least a year;
- a federal offense relating to the prostitution business;
- a federal offense relating to peonage, slavery, involuntary servitude, or trafficking in persons;
- any of various offenses relating to espionage, protecting undercover agents, classified information, sabotage, or treason;
- fraud, deceit, or federal tax evasion, if the offense involves more than $10,000;
- alien smuggling, other than a first offense involving the alien's spouse, child, or parent;
- illegal entry or reentry of an alien previously deported on account of committing an aggravated felony;
- an offense relating to falsely making, forging, counterfeiting, mutilating, or altering a passport or immigration document if (1) the term of imprisonment is at least a year and (2) the offense is not a first offense relating to the alien's spouse, parent, or child;
- failure to appear for service of a sentence, if the underlying offense is punishable by imprisonment of at least five years;
- an offense relating to commercial bribery, counterfeiting, forgery, or trafficking in vehicles with altered identification numbers, for which the term of imprisonment is at least one year;
- an offense relating to obstruction of justice, perjury or subornation of perjury, or bribery of a witness, for which the term of imprisonment is at least one year;

- an offense relating to a failure to appear before a court pursuant to a court order to answer to or dispose of a charge of a felony for which a sentence of two years' imprisonment or more may be imposed; and
- an attempt or conspiracy to commit one of the foregoing offenses.

Unless otherwise specified, an aggravated felony includes both state and federal convictions, as well as foreign convictions for which the term of imprisonment was completed less than 15 years earlier.[19]

Crimes Affecting Assessment of Good Moral Character

The possession of good moral character appears always to have been a statutory requirement for naturalization,[20] and good moral character now also bears on the eligibility for various forms of immigration relief.[21] Prior to 1952, the effect of criminal conduct upon assessments of good moral character was determined solely by case law and administrative practice. Following the enactment of the INA, certain criminal activities were statutorily designated as barring a finding of good moral character. The activities listed by the INA as prohibiting a finding of good moral character are not exclusive, and engaging in illegal activity that is not specifically designated by the INA may therefore still be considered when assessing character.[22]

Although not every activity listed by the INA as barring a finding of good moral character directly relates to illegal behavior,[23] most do. Pursuant to INA § 101(f), an alien is barred from being found to have good moral character if, during the period for which character is required to be established,[24] the alien

- commits certain acts related to prostitution or another commercialized vice;
- knowingly encourages, induces, assists, abets, or aids any other alien to enter or to try to enter the United States in violation of law, except in limited circumstances;
- commits a crime of moral turpitude, unless the alien committed only one crime and either (1) the crime was committed while the alien was a minor and the crime (as well as the alien's release from any imprisonment for the crime) occurred at least five years prior to the pertinent application or (2) the maximum possible penalty for the crime did not exceed one year's imprisonment and the sentence imposed did not exceed six months;

- violates a federal, state, or foreign law or regulation relating to a controlled substance, other than a single offense of possessing 30 grams or less of marijuana;
- commits two or more offenses for which the aggregate sentence imposed was at least five years;
- gives false information in attempting to receive a benefit under the INA;
- has an income principally derived from illegal gambling activities;
- commits at least two gambling offenses for which the alien is convicted;
- is in criminal confinement for at least 180 days; or
- has *at any time* been convicted of an aggravated felony.[25]

As previously mentioned, the INA's listing of conduct barring a finding of good moral character is not exclusive, and other activities—criminal or otherwise—may also bar an alien from citizenship or immigration benefits on character grounds. Among potential disqualifying conduct are an alien's deliberate non-support of his or her family, adultery that tended to destroy an existing marriage, and other notorious unlawful conduct.[26] Additionally, crimes committed before the "good moral character" period may be considered.[27]

MAJOR IMMIGRATION CONSEQUENCES FOR CRIMINAL ALIENS

Certain criminal conduct may have a substantial impact upon an alien's ability to enter or remain in the United States, and it may also affect the availability of discretionary forms of immigration relief and the ability of an alien to become a U.S. citizen. The following sections describe the major immigration consequences for aliens who engage in certain criminal conduct.

Designation As Inadmissible Alien

The INA categorizes certain classes of aliens as inadmissible, making them "ineligible to receive visas and ineligible to be admitted to the United

States."[28] Aliens who commit certain crimes are designated as inadmissible. Aliens designated as inadmissible include any alien who, *inter alia*

- has been convicted of, admits having committed, or admits to acts comprising essential elements of a crime involving moral turpitude (other than a purely political offense), unless (1) the alien committed only one crime and (2)(a) the crime was committed when the alien was under the age of 18 and the crime was committed (and any related incarceration ended) more than five years prior to the application for admission or for a visa or (b) the maximum penalty for the crime at issue did not exceed one year's imprisonment and, if convicted, the alien was not sentenced to more than six months;
- has been convicted of, admits having committed, or admits to acts comprising essential elements of a federal, state, or foreign law violation relating to a controlled substance;
- based on the knowledge or reasonable belief of a consular officer or immigration officer, (1) is or has been an illicit trafficker in a controlled substance, or knowingly is or has been an aider or abettor of a controlled substance, or (2) is the spouse, son, or daughter of an alien inadmissible for the foregoing reasons, and has, within the previous five years, obtained any financial or other benefit from the illicit activity of that alien, and knew or reasonably should have known that the financial or other benefit was the product of such illicit activity;
- has been convicted of two or more offenses for which the aggregate sentence imposed was at least five years;
- is coming to the United States to engage in (or within 10 years of applying for admission has engaged in) prostitution (including procurement and receipt of proceeds) or is coming to the United States to engage in another form of unlawful commercialized vice;
- committed a serious crime for which diplomatic immunity or other form of immunity was claimed;
- (1) commits or has conspired to commit a human trafficking offense, either in or outside the United States, or is known or reasonably believed to have aided or otherwise furthered severe forms of human trafficking or (2) is known or reasonably believed to be the adult child or spouse of such an alien and knowingly benefitted from the proceeds of illicit activity while an adult in the past 5 years;

- based on the knowledge or reasonable belief of a consular officer or immigration officer, is engaging, or seeks to enter the United States to engage, in a federal offense of money laundering, or is or has been a knowing aider, abettor, assister, conspirator, or colluder with others in such an offense; or
- based on the knowledge or reasonable belief of a consular officer or immigration officer, seeks to enter the United States to engage in espionage, sabotage, export control violations, unlawful opposition to the government, or other unlawful activity.[29]

Other types of unlawful conduct (which may also be covered under criminal grounds) precluding admission include terrorist activities, alien smuggling (with limited exception), immigration document fraud, illegal entry into the United States, unlawful voting, international abduction of a child who is a U.S. citizen, participation in genocide, recruitment of child soldiers, and severe violations of religious freedom while serving as a foreign government official.

Waivers

Various criminal grounds for inadmissibility are, by their own terms, subject to exception. For example, the crime of moral turpitude category does not cover certain juvenile or minor offenses.[30] Further, even if a crime is covered, most criminal grounds for inadmissibility may nevertheless be waived in a number of circumstances. Authority to waive certain criminal grounds of inadmissibility is contained in INA § 212(h).[31] Criminal grounds for inadmissibility that may be waived are

- crimes involving moral turpitude;
- a single offense of simple possession of 30 grams or less of marijuana;
- multiple convictions for which at least five year's imprisonment was imposed;
- prostitution or other unlawful commercialized vices; and
- serious criminal activity for which the alien has asserted immunity.

INA § 212(h)(1) establishes that relevant immigration officials have discretion to waive a designation of inadmissibility on account of the foregoing conduct if four requirements are met. These requirements are that

- the alien is seeking admission as an LPR;
- the conduct making the alien inadmissible either involved prostitution or another unlawful commercial vice or, in the case of other criminal conduct, occurred more than 15 years before the date of the alien's application for a visa, entry or adjustment of status;
- the alien's admission into the United States would not be contrary to the national welfare, safety, or security of the United States; *and*
- the alien has been rehabilitated.[32]

An additional waiver is available for immediate family members under INA § 212(h)(1)(B) if

- the alien is seeking admission as an LPR;
- the alien is the spouse, parent, son, or daughter of a U.S. citizen or LPR; *and*
- denial of admission would cause extreme hardship to the United States citizen or lawfully resident spouse, parent, son, or daughter.[33]

A further circumstance where a waiver is available for inadmissible criminal conduct involves alien spouses or children of U.S. citizens or LPRs, when those aliens have been battered or subjected to extreme cruelty by the citizen or LPR.[34]

Certain aliens are barred from consideration for § 212(h) waivers. No waiver is permitted for aliens who have been convicted of murder or criminal acts involving torture, as well as attempts or conspiracies to commit murder or a criminal act involving torture.[35] Further, a waiver under § 212(h) is not available in the case of an alien who has previously been admitted to the United States as an LPR if either (1) since the date of such admission the alien has been convicted of an aggravated felony or (2) the alien has not lawfully resided continuously in the United States for at least seven years immediately preceding the date of initiation of proceedings to remove the alien from the United States.[36]

In addition to § 212(h) waivers, criminal grounds may be waived for aliens seeking temporary admission as nonimmigrants, such as those seeking to enter the United States as tourists.[37] Also, certain permanent residents may seek waivers through cancellation of removal, which will be discussed later.[38]

Deportation

The criminal grounds for deportation cover both broad categories and specific crimes. Among those deportable on criminal grounds is any alien who

- is convicted of a single crime involving moral turpitude that was committed within five years of admission and that is punishable by imprisonment of at least one year;
- is convicted of two or more crimes involving moral turpitude not arising from a single scheme of misconduct;
- is convicted of an aggravated felony at any time after admission into the United States;
- is convicted of failing to register as a sex offender;
- is convicted after admission of any violation of a federal, state, or foreign law or regulation relating to a controlled substance (other than a single offense for possessing 30 grams or less of marijuana for personal use);
- is, or at any time after admission has been, a drug abuser or drug addict;
- is convicted at any time after admission of an offense related to a firearm or destructive device (including unlawful commerce relating to, possession, or use of a firearm or destructive device);
- is convicted at any time of an offense related to espionage, sabotage, or treason or sedition, if the offense is punishable by imprisonment of five years or more;
- is convicted of an offense under the Military Selective Service Act or the Trading with the Enemy Act;
- is convicted of an offense under 18 U.S.C. § 758 (high-speed flight from an immigration checkpoint);
- is convicted of an offense related to launching an expedition against a country with which the United States is at peace;
- is convicted of threatening by mail the President, Vice President, or other officer in the line of presidential succession;
- is convicted at any time after entry of a crime of domestic violence, stalking, child abuse, child neglect, or child abandonment;
- violates a protection order related to violence or harassment; or
- is described in the ground for inadmissibility relating to human trafficking offenses.[39]

Waivers

Crimes involving moral turpitude, aggravated felonies, and high-speed flight from an immigration checkpoint may all be automatically waived as grounds for deportation upon the alien receiving a full and unconditional pardon by the President or governor.[40] *Cancellation of removal* as a form of discretionary relief, which is discussed below, and *§ 212(h) waivers of inadmissibility*, which are discussed above, may also be relevant in deportation cases.

Denial of Discretionary Relief

In addition to providing for discretionary waivers, the INA provides designated immigration authorities with the power to grant an alien asylum, cancel removal proceedings against him, permit his voluntary departure from the United States, or adjust the alien's status under registry provisions. However, authority to grant these remedies is circumscribed with respect to certain types of criminal aliens.

Asylum

Although asylum is a discretionary remedy for aliens who face persecution, it is unavailable to an alien who (1) "[h]aving been convicted ... of a particularly serious crime" (including an aggravated felony[41] or an offense designated by the Attorney General as "particularly serious"), constitutes a danger to the community;" or (2) is reasonably believed to have committed a serious nonpolitical offense outside the United States (including such offenses as may be designated by the Attorney General).[42] P.L. 110-340 requires the Attorney General and Secretary of Homeland Security to promulgate regulations establishing that persons inadmissible or deportable on account of recruiting child soldiers in violation of federal law have committed a serious nonpolitical crime making them ineligible for asylum. Further, an alien who is involved in specified terrorist activities, is a danger to national security, or has engaged in persecution of any person on account of race, religion, nationality, political opinion or membership in a particular social group is also ineligible for asylum.[43]

Withholding of Removal

Apart from asylum is the separate remedy of *withholding of removal*. Like asylum, withholding of removal is premised upon a showing of prospective persecution of an alien if removed to a particular country.[44] Withholding of removal differs from asylum in (1) requiring a higher standard of proof; (2) limiting relief to the claimant (as opposed to also including the claimant's spouse and minor children); (3) failing to allow for adjustment to LPR status; and (4) being a mandatory rather than discretionary form of relief for qualifying aliens. Although the remedy of withholding is stated in mandatory terms, otherwise eligible aliens are, with limited exception, disqualified under criminal grounds similar to those that apply to asylum.[45] The primary difference, however, is that not all aggravated felonies automatically bar withholding of removal. Instead, relief is barred only if the alien has been convicted of one or more aggravated felonies for which the aggregate sentence imposed was five years or more.

Cancellation of Removal

In 1996, the INA was amended to combine two types of discretionary relief for long-term alien residents—"*§ 212(c)" relief* for LPRs who had resided in the U.S. for an extended period and *suspension of deportation* for other long-term aliens—into a new remedy called *cancellation of removal.* Cancellation of removal, in turn, maintains some of the distinctions that appeared under the forms of relief that preceded it.

Under provisions corresponding with earlier INA provisions concerning *suspension of deportation*, the Attorney General may cancel the removal of certain otherwise inadmissible or deportable non-LPRs if they have been in the United States continuously for at least 10 years and their removal would result in exceptional and extremely unusual hardship for immediate family members.[47] However, certain criminal activity makes an alien ineligible for cancellation of removal despite whatever roots the alien has established in the United States. Disqualifying criminal activity includes convictions of crimes that preclude a finding of good moral character and crimes that fall within the criminal grounds for inadmissibility or deportation.[48] Civil immigration document fraud also precludes relief.[49] Additionally, "continuous residence" for purposes of qualifying for relief stops on the *commission* of an offense that would render the alien inadmissible.[50]

Under provisions that correspond to *relief previously available under INA § 212(c)*, the Attorney General may cancel the removal of an alien who has been an LPR for at least five years, if the alien has resided in the United States continuously for at least seven years and has not been convicted of an aggravated felony.[51] Further, "continuous residence" for purposes of qualifying for relief stops upon the *commission* of an offense that would render the alien inadmissible.[52]

Voluntary Departure

Through a grant of voluntary departure, an otherwise deportable alien may depart the United States without the stigma and legal consequences that would attach to a compulsory removal order. There are two standards for voluntary departure, depending on whether permission to leave voluntarily is sought before or after removal proceedings against the alien are completed. If voluntary departure is sought before proceedings are initiated (e.g., upon the alien being arrested by an immigration enforcement officer) or completed, the only criminal disqualification is for conviction of an aggravated felony (terrorist activities are also disqualifying).[53] If voluntary departure is sought after removal proceedings are completed, the alien must not have been convicted of an aggravated felony and must also have been a person of good moral character for at least five years preceding.[54]

Temporary Protected Status

In order to qualify for asylum or withholding of removal, an alien must show that he or she would personally face persecution. Aliens whose lives have been disrupted by generalized violence or natural disaster may not qualify on that basis alone. However, the INA permits temporary haven for nationals of countries that have been designated as experiencing widespread upheaval.[55] At the same time, relief is granted on an individual basis, and an otherwise eligible alien shall be denied protection if he or she is inadmissible on criminal grounds related to (1) crimes involving moral turpitude, (2) multiple criminal convictions, (3) or drug offenses (other than a single offense for possessing 30 grams or less of marijuana).[56] Additional, overlapping categories of aliens who are disqualified from receiving temporary protected status are those who (1) have been convicted of one felony or two or more misdemeanors in the United States or (2) who would be disqualified from asylum due to criminal conduct.[57]

Adjustment of Status

Under certain circumstances, an alien with nonimmigrant status may adjust to LPR status.[58] Certain aliens without legal status may also adjust if they had a preference petition or labor certification application filed on their behalf as of April 30, 2001, or under certain other circumstances.[59] Otherwise eligible aliens are barred from adjustment if they are inadmissible, including those who are inadmissible on criminal grounds.

Registry

The INA has long contained authority for the adjustment to LPR status for aliens who have lived in the United States for an extended period. Known as the registry provision,[60] this authority now allows for the adjustment of aliens who have lived in the United States since before 1972.[61] However, aliens who are inadmissible on criminal grounds are ineligible for adjustment, as are aliens who lack good moral character.[62]

Naturalization Restrictions

An essential requirement for becoming a U.S. citizen through naturalization is that the applicant establish that he or she has been, and continues to be, a person of good moral character.[63] An LPR seeking naturalization is required to maintain good moral character for *at least five years* preceding his or her application for naturalization; five years being the minimum period of time that a person lawfully admitted into the United States must continuously reside in the country before applying for naturalization.[64]

As discussed previously, certain criminal acts may disqualify an alien from being found to possess good moral character.[65] Pursuant to INA § 101(f), certain listed categories of criminal conduct automatically preclude an alien from being found to possess good moral character. This listing is not exclusive, and other conduct—criminal or otherwise—may also prevent a finding of good moral character, including crimes that occur before the statutory period requiring "good moral character" actually begins. For a more detailed discussion of the crimes that preclude a finding of good moral character, refer to the section of this report entitled *Crimes Affecting Assessment of Good Moral Character*.

RECENT LEGISLATIVE ACTIVITY

In recent years, numerous proposals have been introduced to modify the immigration consequences of criminal activity. The 110th Congress enacted several such measures, including P.L. 110-257, providing certain relief from inadmissibility to members of the African National Congress; P.L. 110-340, making persons who have engaged in the recruitment of child soldiers in violation of federal law inadmissible, deportable and ineligible for asylum or withholding of removal; and P.L. 110-457, modifying the grounds for inadmissibility and removal related to human trafficking.

It is possible that proposals will be introduced in the 111th Congress to further modify the immigration consequences of criminal activity. Proposals made in recent years that have received legislative action or significant congressional interest include measures that would:

- add further document-fraud offenses to the list of criminal activities making aliens inadmissible and/or deportable;
- make gang-related activity a ground for inadmissibility, deportation, and ineligibility from certain forms of relief from removal;
- make DUI offenses a ground for inadmissibility or deportation; and
- specify that an aggravated felony conviction is a ground for inadmissibility.[66]

End Notes

[1] For further background on U.S. immigration policy, see CRS Report RS20916, *Immigration and Naturalization Fundamentals*, by Ruth Ellen Wasem.

[2] 8 U.S.C. §§ 1101 *et seq.*

[3] INA § 101(a)(15)(F); 8 U.S.C. § 1101(a)(15)(F).

[4] 8 U.S.C. § 1182.

[5] 8 U.S.C. § 1227.

[6] *See* INA §§ 212(a)(2) 237(a)(2); 8 U.S.C. §§ 1182(a)(2), 1227(a)(2).

[7] Unlawful presence is only a criminal offense when an alien is found in the United States after having been formally removed or after departing the United States while a removal order was outstanding. INA § 276; 8 U.S.C. § 1326. questions of immigration law.

[8] Primary authority over immigration matters was transferred from the Department of Labor to the Department of Justice in 1940. Reorg. Plan No. 5 of 1940, 5 Fed. Reg. 2223 (1940).

[9] 8 U.S.C. § 1103(a)(1).

[10] *Id.* at § 1103(a)(1), (g).

[11] For further background on the transfer of immigration authority to the DHS, see CRS Report RL31997, *Authority to Enforce the Immigration and Nationality Act (INA) in the Wake of the Homeland Security Act: Legal Issues*, by Stephen R. Vina.

[12] According to the DOJ, which issued these regulations just prior to the transfer of certain immigration authority to the DHS, the duplication of regulations was intended "to ensure continuity, even though the Attorney General and Secretary may later amend their respective regulations to further separate the procedures and clarify those sections that affect each agency ... [but] the duplication assures that interpretation will be consistent until coordinated decisions are made respecting these procedures." Department of Justice, Final

Rule, Aliens and Nationality; Homeland Security; Reorganization of Regulations, 68 Fed. Reg. 9824, 9825 (February 28, 2003) (codified at 8 C.F.R pts. I, V).

[13] Homeland Security Act of 2002, P.L. 107-296, § 456.

[14] For example, *crimes involving moral turpitude* that may make an alien *inadmissible* include all such crimes other than (1) a single such crime committed by a minor if the crime was committed, and any confinement ended, at least five years before applying for admission or (2) a single misdemeanor for which the term of imprisonment imposed, if any, did not exceed six months. INA § 212(a)(2)(A); 8 U.S.C. § 1182(a)(2)(A). On the other hand, *crimes involving moral turpitude* that may make an alien *deportable* include (1) one conviction of such a crime committed within five years of entry (ten years in the case of a small subcategory of aliens) if the crime is punishable by at least one year's imprisonment, and (2) the conviction of more than one such crime, whenever committed and whatever the potential punishment, if the crimes were not committed in a single scheme of criminal conduct. INA § 237(a)(2)(A); § 8 U.S.C. § 1227(a)(2)(A).

[15] Prior to 1891, conviction of a "felonious crime" served as the basis of exclusion. Subsequently, conviction for a "felony or other infamous crime or misdemeanor involving moral turpitude" could constitute grounds for alien exclusion. Act of March 3, 1891, 26 Stat. 1084, ch. 551.

[16] For a more thorough listing of crimes found to involve moral turpitude, see Maryellen Fullerton & Noah Kinigstein, *Strategies for Ameliorating the Immigration Consequences of Criminal Convictions: A Guide for Defense Attorneys*, 23 AM. CRIM. L. REV. 425, 431-36 (1986).

[17] P.L. 100-690 (1988).

[18] *See id.* at § 7342.

[19] INA § 101(a)(43); 8 U.S.C. § 1101(a)(43).

[20] Possession of "good moral character" was a requirement for naturalization under the original U.S. naturalization law. Act of March 26, 1790, 1 Stat 103-104.

[21] For a more detailed discussion of good moral character, see 7 CHARLES GORDON, STANLEY MAILMAN & STEPHEN YALE-LOEHR, 7 IMMIGRATION LAW & PROCEDURE § 95.04[1] (2002) [*hereinafter* "GORDON & MAILMAN"].

[22] *See* 8 C.F.R. § 316.10(a)(2) (stating that naturalization officials "evaluate claims of good moral character on a case-by-case basis taking into account the elements enumerated [under the INA and corresponding regulations] ... and the standards of the average citizen in the community of residence").

[23] For example, an alien determined to be a habitual drunkard is statutorily barred from being considered to possess good moral character. INA § 101(f)(1); 8 U.S.C. § 1101(f)(1).

[24] The INA imposes different requirements on an alien to demonstrate good moral character depending upon what benefit he or she is seeking. For example, most LPRs petitioning for naturalization must have resided in the United States for at least five years and have shown good moral character during this period. INA § 316(a); 8 U.S.C. § 1427(a). For a non-LPR alien to be eligible for cancellation of removal from the United States, he or she must have had a continuous presence in the United States for at least 10 years and good moral character during that period. INA § 240A(b)(1); 8 U.S.C. § 1229b(b)(1).

[25] However, a conviction for an aggravated felony before November 29, 1990 (other than for murder) does not automatically preclude a finding of good moral character under INA § 101(f). 8 C.F.R. § 316.60(b)(1).

[26] *Id.* at § 316.60(b)(3). *See generally* GORDON & MAILMAN, *supra* note 21, § 95.04[1][b].

[27] 8 C.F.R. § 316.60(a)(2).

[28] INA § 212(a); 8 U.S.C. § 1182(a).
[29] INA § 212(a); 8 U.S.C. § 1182(a).
[30] INA § 212(a)(2)(A)(ii); 8 U.S.C. § 1182(a)(2)(A)(ii).
[31] 8 U.S.C. § 1182(h).
[32] INA § 212(h)(1)(A); 8 U.S.C. § 1182(h)(1)(A).
[33] 8 U.S.C. § 1182(h)(1)(B).
[34] INA § 212(h)(1)(C); 8 U.S.C. § 1182(h)(1)(C).
[35] 8 U.S.C. § 1182(h).
[36] *Id.*
[37] INA § 212(d)(3); 8 U.S.C. § 1182(d)(3).
[38] *See infra* at 12-13.
[39] INA § 237(a)(2); 8 U.S.C. § 1227(a)(2).
[40] INA § 237(a)(2)(A)(v); 8 U.S.C. § 1227(a)(2)(A)(v).
[41] For purposes of § 208, an alien who has been convicted of an aggravated felony is considered to have been convicted of a particularly serious crime. INA § 208(b)(2)(B)(i); 8 U.S.C. § 1158(b)(2)(B)(i).
[42] INA § 208(b)(2); 8 U.S.C. § 1158(b)(2).
[43] INA § 208(b)(2); 8 U.S.C. § 1158(b)(2).
[44] *See* INA § 241(b)(3); 8 U.S.C. § 1231(b)(3). *See also* 8 C.F.R. § 208.16.
[45] INA § 241(b)(3)(B); 8 U.S.C. § 1231(b)(3)(B). However, under regulations implementing the United Nations Convention Against Torture, no alien is permitted be removed to a country when it is more likely than not that he would face torture there, regardless of whether he or she would be otherwise ineligible for withholding of removal. 8 C.F.R. §§ 208.16-18, 1208.16-18.
[46] INA § 241(b)(3); 8 U.S.C. § 1231(b)(3).
[47] INA § 240A(b)(1); 8 U.S.C. § 1229b(b)(1).
[48] INA §§ 240A(b)(1)(B)-(C); 8 U.S.C. §§ 1229b(b)(1)(B)-(C).
[49] INA § 240A(b)(1)(C); 8 U.S.C. § 1229b(b)(1)(C).
[50] INA § 240A(d); 8 U.S.C. § 1229b(d).
[51] INA § 240A(a); 8 U.S.C. § 1229b(a).
[52] INA § 240A(d); 8 U.S.C. § 1229b(d).
[53] INA § 240B(a)(1); 8 U.S.C. § 1229c(a)(1).
[54] INA § 240B(b)(1); 8 U.S.C. § 1229c(b)(1).
[55] INA § 244; 8 U.S.C. § 1254a. For further background on the availability of temporary protected status for certain aliens, see CRS Report RS20844, *Temporary Protected Status: Current Immigration Policy and Issues*, by Ruth Ellen Wasem and Karma Ester.
[56] INA § 244(c)(2)(A); 8 U.S.C. § 1254a(c)(2)(A).
[57] INA § 244(c)(2)(B); 8 U.S.C. § 1254a(c)(2)(B).
[58] INA § 245; 8 U.S.C. § 1255. *See generally* CRS Report RL32235, *U.S. Immigration Policy on Permanent Admissions*, by Ruth Ellen Wasem.
[59] INA § 245(i)(1); 8 U.S.C. § 1255(i)(1).
[60] A more detailed explanation on the registry provision can be found in CRS Report RL30578, *Immigration: Registry as Means of Obtaining Lawful Permanent Residence*, by Andorra Bruno.
[61] INA § 249; 8 U.S.C. § 1259.
[62] INA § 249; 8 U.S.C. § 1259.
[63] INA § 316; 8 U.S.C. § 1427.
[64] INA § 316(a); 8 U.S.C. § 1427(a).

[65] *See supra* at 5-7.

[66] See, e.g., S. 1348, S. 1639, S.Amdt. 1150 to S. 1348, 110th Cong.; House-passed H.R. 4437, Senate-passed S. 2611, 109th Cong.

INDEX

#

A

B

C

D

E

F

G

H

I

S

T